#TeacherTired

Spiritual Strength Training for the Teacher Heart

Gina Rodriguez

UNITED H

ISBN: 978-1-952840-02-9

UNITED HOUSE Publishing
Waterford, Michigan
info@unitedhousepublishing.com
www.unitedhousepublishing.com

Cover and interior design: Matt Russell, Marketing Image, mrussell@marketing-image.com

Printed in the United States of America
2020—First Edition

SPECIAL SALES
Most UNITED HOUSE books are available at special quantity discounts when purchased in bulk by corporations, organizations, and special-interest groups. For information, please e-mail orders@

#DedicatedTo

To my arrows, your mom finally did it. I am stepping out to cast my stone across the waters, praying that you will believe any gift given from above is a gift given to create ripples in the lives of others. Set your aim high and keep pointing to The One who makes life worth living.

#Endorsements

"You told your story, you described your journey, and even after 37 years in education serving at all levels, I recognized that it was my story too. I know that so many others will feel the same way."- **Carolyn Copelin Foxx**: 37 years experience in education at all levels: classroom educator, administrator, speech therapist, educational consultant, countless levels of service.

"As an educator, you will soak up Gina's words and encouragement. She speaks the language of an impassioned, tired educator who wants the very best for her scholars. She brings God into every aspect of her teaching, from setting foot in her classroom the first workday in the fall until the very last box is packed up in the spring. Navigating the world of teaching with God by her side, Gina shares her wisdom with you over and over in this devotional. If you're #teachertired, pick this up and let it speak to your heart and soul, and watch God work!" - **Elisa Preston**: 10 years in education, school counselor, published author

"The experiences shared are authentic. The author shares her spiritual beliefs and struggles with our teaching profession. By God's grace she sees the light and finds strength through the relationships she develops with God and her peers. If you find yourself in need of a good motivational, spiritual, and over-coming the odds book, then this devotional is a must-read for you!" - **Patricia Cisneros**: 25 years of teaching, making an impact, and mentoring peers.

"#TeacherTired is a creative and innovative guide for teachers at all stages in their professional growth and development. From start to finish, I was en-

amored by the raw honesty of the writer as she seamlessly exposes the joy and struggles of this 'noble profession'. If you need your spirit to be "renewed like the eagles" after a challenging day or a difficult school year, this is that book! At the turn of every page, I am reminded that as educators we are not in this walk alone for He is with us." - **Tanya Crawford**: 15 years of teaching high school and serving in leadership roles.

"#TeacherTired is written for educators trying to keep God and faith at the forefront of their classroom. As a teacher, I enjoyed reading #TeacherTired because it was written by a teacher that has had many of the same classroom experiences that I have. All teachers have had moments where they feel like they need to drop to their knees and pray for guidance. #TeacherTired will help guide you through challenging moments using beautifully written prayers, SMART goals to promote thinking, and connection with Our Heavenly Father." - **Ashleigh Bryant**: 12 years of teaching several elementary grades, 2019-2020 Teacher of the Year

#ForTheOne

This is for the one who teaches. The one who imparts knowledge, facilitates learning, and passes on wisdom through instruction, experience, and modeling. This is for you, the daycare provider or the one leading a Sunday school class. To those teaching in the public or private school sector, this is for you. This is for the one who questions their purpose or effectiveness; for the one who is teacher-tired; for the one who is ready for change but feels stuck. This is for the one who continuously gives a part of themselves to meet the needs of others. Wherever you find yourself, **you** are the one this book is for.

This resource is written to encourage educators to bloom where they are planted. Seeking the Son together, we will discover how His radiation of hope and wisdom will give us the energy, motivation, and desire to finish strong. We may not always feel strong and motivated, but God is our constant. He can help us bloom even in a dry, withered season.

#TableOfContents

#Introduction

"The task of the modern educator is not to cut down jungles, but to irrigate deserts."[1]

C.S.Lewis

It dawned on me recently, God has not been removed from schools. The belief God has been removed from the public sector of any industry is not a factual statement. I realize now it cannot be possible to remove His presence when we as believers represent Him wherever we go. When we are educators grounded in Biblical truths and surrendered to our Holy God, His presence goes with us inside the classroom setting, outside on the playground, and to any space we occupy; including the virtual realm. The truth is, I represent Him everywhere I go. This means as a public-school teacher, I am actually bringing God into schools through my attitude, character, love, and heart to serve those around me. I want what I do to go beyond basic academics, rigor, and standards. I want to touch the core and whole person of each student who crosses my path. I want to impact my sphere of influence because it's exactly what Jesus did. Friends, God has placed you exactly where His love needs to be felt. Even if the workplace feels like a desert, He is more than able to quench our thirst. God has not been kicked out of schools as long as we, the body of believers, step in and show His light in deeds and actions.

Truth be told, I can spend more time complaining and murmuring than I do praying for help and change. I can be so good at venting to friends or coworkers about the challenges I face yet take little or no time to express my concerns to the Lord. More often than not, I spend even less time trying to listen to God's response. Many times, I find myself more inclined to ask God for help with relationships, my family, finances, you know, the 'big' stuff, than to intentionally pray over my heart for teaching. I need to spend more time asking God to bring back purpose, perspective, and passion in my career. If we do not have those three anchors, we may falter and be emotionally drained all year, missing what God intended for us to enjoy and value. Purpose keeps our eyes focused. Perspective helps us move forward. Passion gives us the drive to run our race with excellence. Losing perspective, purpose, or passion may come at different times in life. How we respond in those seasons sets us up as either thriving educators or barely surviving teachers. This devotional aims to arm us with spiritual truths which lead us to focus, freedom, and favor.

As we journey together through this book, my hope and prayer for us is to find a new outlook on our calling and that our work would not negatively consume us but be a place to answer a unique call God has given us as educators. Each chapter will hone in on a topic of concern, a thought, or a feeling we have already faced or may encounter. You may not have experienced some of the scenarios described in this book, but the emotions evoked from the situation may sound all too familiar.

There will be three parts to each devotion:

1. **Devotion (a.k.a. digging deep)**- A passage composed of scriptures intertwined with the daily hustle and grind of teaching experiences. At the end of the reading, there will be **power points** referencing the scriptures discussed. Each chapter is titled with a hashtag to represent our everyday culture, and show there is no mundane task, thought, or event God won't give great attention to. Our seemingly ordinary life can be used to point us to an extraordinary God.

2. **Power Moment**- We will end our reading with prayer together. Yes, there is power in prayer. James 5:16b (NIV, emphasis added) confirms, "The prayer of a righteous person is **powerful** and **effective**."

3. **SMART Goals**- A section to make your own personal SMART goals. As most educators have seen, or will see, we are asked to create goals that are specific, measurable, attainable, realistic, and time-bound. However, since we are including God in all we do, our SMART goals will look a little different (more details to follow in the next chapter).

During our time together, we will learn how to use the sword of the spirit, the Word of God, to slash through strongholds, break insecure character traits, and reveal newness in what may be a dry time in our educational career. Whether you are in a season of drought or on a mountaintop of fresh ideas and motivation, there is only room for growth and insight from this point on. There is no better time to grow as an educator from the inside out than now. Whether this is your first year of teaching or you are twenty-plus years into this race, we are all still growing and learning in grace.

Let us get this journey started with our first action step: **prayer**!

Lord, I thank you for the person reading this book right now. I thank you that what you started in our hearts and lives will continue to be molded and perfected to Your grand purpose. Often, the daily requirements and demands placed on us become too much to carry. Many of us are feeling overworked, overwhelmed, and unsatisfied. There are moments when we wonder if what we are doing makes a difference at all. We question our purpose, impact, and calling. Some of us are apathetic, some have stopped caring, and some wonder if the student loan debt accrued is worth the stress associated with teacher life. Others are planning their next move out of the profession. Many are barely making it, ready to throw in the towel. They are drained and tired. Touch the heart and mind of the person reading this right now. Lord, fill our cups to overflowing so we may serve those You have placed under our guidance. Give us back joy and passion as educators. Let us not waste days feeling stuck, discouraged, or depressed. You, mighty King, are able to make the dry deserts gush forth streams of living water. Lord, bring us water in the deserts of teaching; please refresh us. May our purpose be clear, our perspective transformed, and our passion set on fire. In Jesus' name, amen!

#Purpose

"The reason for which something is done or created or for which something exists. Our aim, intention, a person's sense of resolve."[2]

Webster Dictionary

#TeacherTired

"Every happening, great and small, is a parable whereby God speaks to us, and the art of life is to get the message."[3]

Malcolm Muggeridge

It was my second year of teaching, and it was supposed to be better than the dreaded 'first-year' struggles of a new teacher. They said you only have your first year once and it gets better. Well, not for me. Not. For. Me.

I remember long car rides to work crying and telling God how much I dreaded going to work. I told Him I hated my job. Yes, I used the strong word 'hate' because my heart had sunk so low. I was done with teaching. Done with the cattiness at work. Done with the feeling like I lost control of my classroom. Done with the negative parent support at times. Done with feeling unappreciated. Just DONE!

Why you may ask? I was a fairly new teacher and had many students with behavior issues. We all know even one serious behavioral issue can wreak havoc in the classroom atmosphere, and I had several. I was also dealing with parents who didn't seem to care much for me nor felt I was the "best fit" for their child. Telling a new teacher you don't want your child in their class is like telling them they are unfit at their job and what they do isn't good enough. You don't even have to be a new teacher to get some hurt feelings. With time, we learn to cope with these matters a little better, but the sting is always real.

I had the pressure of trying to teach students how to read, write, do math, have social skills (seriously, you know the list goes on), and, at the same time, attempt to have classroom management with students who made me want to quit almost every day. Don't get me wrong, I did have a sweet class. However, when all of these other challenges were thrown at me, I just couldn't find my footing. I kept slipping more and more into a hole of despair. Friends, I wondered daily if I would be able to continue working in a profession bombarded with heavy expectations, lack of support, and lack of compensation. I questioned why I took out student loans only to feel stressed as I hung on paycheck-to-paycheck, unable to pay off the loans quickly. I battled a mountain of feelings. I felt the pressure of failing parents' expectations, battled negative thoughts, faced struggles within the grade level team, and I was lost, completely lost.

I laid in bed several nights heavy-hearted and full of anxiety, questioning God's call in my life. One night, in particular, I remember lying in bed with lights off as quiet tears streamed down my face. Softly I told my husband, "I don't think I am cut out to be a teacher. I can't do this anymore." I will never forget how shocked he was to hear me say this. He'd seen all of the hard work I put into getting my degree and credentials, and he watched me pour out my heart during unpaid student teaching months, racking up hefty credit card debt putting my two kids in daycare, and wanting more than anything to be hired as a contracted teacher. All of the work. All those hopes. All of the excitement and anticipation, gone.

I will not lie and tell you the year ended well. It was the first time in my life I was relieved when a student was removed from my class. The parents wanted it, which hurt my pride, but this intervention was a gift from God, even if it didn't feel good at the time. That year was also the first time I said goodbye to a class and exhaled out of sheer exhaustion. I was ready to say my goodbyes, and sometimes I feel guilty admitting it, but honestly, there are times when we look back and wonder how we even made it. Right? Can I get a witness?

I am here to tell you if you've ever felt these feelings, you are not alone. If you've ever lost your footing getting your classroom together, you are not alone. And if you have ever questioned your sanity as a teacher, you are not alone. This was a low time in my teaching career, but it was also when true dependence and learning started to form in my heart. I was either going to be a miserable teacher trying to survive in the abyss of hopelessness or beg God for help. I chose to ask God for help. Honestly, I wish I could say it was because I was so 'spiritual' and just knew it was the right thing to do. Truth is, I couldn't afford to quit. Number one, I needed to work, and there was no other choice but to continue showing up. Number two, I was done trying to fix things on my own strength and getting nowhere. Number three, I was lost and so unhappy. The irony of this dilemma was that teaching really was something I had a knack for, something I knew deep down was a gift I had been given, but I couldn't find happiness in it.

Here's the good news, God doesn't waste any challenge, season of pain, or discomfort. There is no wasted time with the Lord. As Malcolm Muggeridge says in the opening thoughts of this chapter, "...the art of life is to get the message." What message can we gain from those challenges we face? There is growth and refinement when we use these seasons to build a stronger relationship with our Lord and Savior. The problem is, instead of running to Him for help, we often dig our heels in a little deeper and try to figure things out on our own. Friends, I am here to give testimony to how God can turn things around and grant favor over our careers because He can do the impossible.

The times we find ourselves barely hanging on and forcing ourselves to go to work are the times we need serious intervention to bring us back to a place where we have passion, belief in our purpose, and to find joy again in what we do. I look back on that year with great appreciation. I learned the hard way what it means to be in the trenches of what we do. God was showing me early in my career, not every year will be the same, not everything will be rainbows and butterflies, and not everyone will approve of or like me. I needed to learn the importance of praying over my classroom and students, renewing my mind, and taking the time to pray over my future students and their parents. I prayed for favor. I prayed I would get students who needed me and my style of teaching and which students I needed to help me learn and grow. That year taught me I never wanted to leave my future, my class, or my happiness to chance. I became a huge advocate for praying over my calling and praying over everyone God would place in my path.

I realized then, I needed to include God in all aspects of my life. Including God in my life needs to be evident in all I do, even in teaching. Maybe some of you reading already do this. You pray for your class. You pray for your school, administration, students, parents, lessons, ideas, and for favor and positive interactions with others; that's great! However, if you are like me in my early teaching days, you may not be in the habit of doing so. I encourage you to remember what Romans 8:26 (AMP) says, "In the same way the Spirit [comes to us and] helps us in our weakness. We do not know what prayer to offer *or* how to offer it as we should, but the Spirit Himself [knows our need and at the right time] intercedes on our behalf with sighs *and* groanings too deep for words."

Friends, we do not need to know the exact words to pray. God already knows our deepest need. He promises to help us in our weakness; it says so right there in His Word. All we need to do is go to Him, speak from our heart, and in moments where we have no words, have no fear, the Bible says the Holy Spirit makes intercession on our behalf. Wow. What a wonderful God we serve. We don't have to have it all together to go to The One who does. Romans 8:28 (AMP) declares, "And we know [with great confidence] that God [who is deeply concerned about us] causes all things to work together [as a plan] for good for those who love God, to those who are called according to His plan *and* purpose." We have a plan and a purpose. God has given us a higher purpose for what we do as educators. We represent His love. We are workers in a much-needed mission field. We have the opportunity to bridge gaps in learning, enhance motivation, and help those who are discouraged. If we see our purpose as more than just checking off standards and following a pacing guide, it will help us continue even when we don't 'feel' like it.

There is no other teacher like you. God knows this, and you need to know it. No one else can give the care, insight, depth of knowledge, or impact you can. We bring hope to learners and those we meet. We've been created and positioned purposefully to be the salt of the earth (Mattew 5:13 ESV) and add our unique flavor to the world around us. We are teachers. Let us not allow #teachertired to define us. I am not saying we won't ever get tired, weary, or have moments of insanity; that's called life. However, let's cling to some powerful words of knowledge, words sharper than a double-edged sword, words that will help cut us loose from the tight grip of tension the daily grind can bring. His perspective and truths will empower us to be the light to a profession in need of change. Galatians 6:9 (NIV) tells us, "Let us not become weary in doing good, for at the proper time, we will reap a harvest if we do not give up."

POWER POINTS

Romans 8:26
Romans 8:28
Galatians 6:9
Matthew 5:13

POWER MOMENT

God, you are the only one who truly knows each and every need. You know how one crazy, overwhelming workday can leave me feeling completely drained and dead inside. However, just as You told the Prophet Ezekiel to "Prophesy to these bones and say to them, 'Dry bones, hear the word of the Lord,'" I also speak to my dry soul and bones to hear and listen to the word of the Lord (Ezekiel 37:4, NIV). Your Word says You will hear my prayers. Your Word says at the proper time, I will reap a harvest if I do not give up. Lord, give me the strength, energy, and motivation to continue forward with excellence. May I do so with such grace that I will be overwhelmed at the new and refreshing moments I will experience. Lord, take my #teachertired heart and help me live on purpose for the purpose You have called me. Make what seems impossible to me, possible. In Jesus' name, amen!

SMART GOALS

This section of SMART goals will be at the end of each chapter. Take time and ask the Holy Spirit to help you select a verse from the power points that you can remember, reflect on, and/or put into practice. The next series of prompts is your journal space to write your thoughts and reflections. Feel free to put pen to paper and express any revelations or insight you may have after each chapter reading.

Select - Choose a verse to meditate on from the chapter. Write it below.

_____

_____

_____

Marinate - Once you have chosen a verse, let it sink into your spirit. What thoughts or impressions do you feel the Holy Spirit is revealing to you?

_____

_____

_____

Ask - Ask God for clarity and wisdom as you finish up the day's reading. Ask what He would like you to do or improve. Ask Him for help if there's an area of need or a way you can bless someone else in need.

_____

_____

_____

Reveal - What has God revealed to you during this devotional time? Write down any thoughts or revelations.

_____

_____

_____

Take Action - What is a practical step you can take after reading today's chapter or selected verse?

_____

_____

_____

#TheGodWhoSeesMe

"What comes into our minds when we think about God is the most important thing about us."[4]

A.W. Tozer

One of the challenges in writing this devotional was bypassing my fear of rejection and falling short of my goal to help educators get grounded, rejuvenated, and encouraged by God's Word. My heart desired to create a study to help fellow teachers fill their tanks with hope, strength, and comfort; however, I had to accept that maybe the person who needed the reminders and reassurance was myself. How could I share a message of hope and joy when I was questioning how much longer I could continue in this profession or when I was questioning my own purpose?

I have been a teacher for over ten years. I have seen how hard educators work: the never-ending pendulum swings and an absurd amount of 'new' strategies we are told to try but never really get good at because they change so quickly. I've learned more 'new' strategies which are really old strategies with a new name. I have sat in 'professional development' meetings intended to unpack standards (over and over and over…) yet longed for professional development which showed ways to actually implement best practices. I have been told to do something one way, only to be bombarded with yet another new plan of action more times than I can count. I have had to use and modify 'teacher lingo' several times. For example, it's not "standard," it's "objective." Nope, now it's a "goal." No, actually it's a "learning target." Wait, scratch that; it's a "focus point." Do you get where I am going with this? Sometimes, we as educators get to a point where we are not only tired but brain-fried from all of the other expectations placed on our plate. Somewhere along the way, the actual teaching experience got lost in the shuffle of finding the latest trend or research-based practice. To top off the already imbalanced load of work, we have some (maybe many) crazy, no good, horrible, rotten kind of days which leave us winded before the day is through. We feel stuck, unseen, and unheard.

Maybe the one person who needs the reminder, "You are seen and heard," is me. Maybe, it's you too. So, how does one find hope in this situation? How does one see the light at the end of the tunnel? The answer: **El Roi**, meaning, **"The God Who Sees Me."**

Let me explain.

Better yet, let's look to the Word of God. Exodus 2:24-25 (MSG) describes:

> *God listened to their groanings.*
> *God remembered His covenant with Abraham, with Isaac, and with Jacob.*
> *God saw what was going on with Israel.*
> *God understood.*

Verse 25 of the Amplified Bible states, "God saw the sons of Israel, and God took notice [of them] *and* was concerned about them [knowing all, understanding all, remembering all]."

You see, Israel was being led by a spiteful Egyptian king who abused his power, mistreated the Israelites, and kept them in captivity. After so much groaning and complaining, these verses show that God **listened** to their groanings. Yes, He even hears our groanings. There are moments in our lives when words do no justice to what we are experiencing or feeling. There are times when "groaning" may be all we can release.

There have been days I literally groaned for rest and calm. There have been days (many days) where I was barely making it out of the classroom door on time, trying to dismiss the students, exhausted, and stressed out because of behavior issues and feeling like I spent most of my day redirecting yet failing to get a handle on things. Groaning. Can you hear it? Been there?

The beautiful takeaway from the verses above is how God listened to their groaning. He saw what was going on and He understood. Friends, the Word says, "Jesus Christ is the same yesterday and today and forever" (Hebrews 13:8, NIV). If He can hear groanings and see the need in the past, then He can hear and see our situation in the present. How much more will He help us now when we are intentional and ask Him to intervene? God sees us in the classroom. He sees us arriving early and staying late. He sees us stressed out trying to keep up with timelines, pacing guides, curriculum, parent phone calls and emails, and students with their individual needs to meet. He sees how tired we are and how hurt we may feel when there is a complaint sent out against us. He sees all of the extra 'little' things we prepare and do to get ready for our days. He sees the lessons and the purchases for our classrooms. He sees us one step away from calling it quits, unable to do so for whatever reason. He sees the struggle, and He understands. He sees it all.

God gave us His Word to see His power, authority, and hand move in the lives of those in the Bible. This was done not just to be a story we read but to remind us He is near. It is a glimpse into His character. Just as God saw and acted to bring relief to the Israelites, I believe God is ready and able to bring relief to those of us who are in need. God sees a whole nation cry for help, but He also sees the silent cries of one teacher ready to throw in the towel. He sees me, and He sees you. Whether on the mountain top or valley low, He sees us. The issue is: Do we believe this when we think of Him? Do we wholeheartedly believe God sees us and will act on our behalf?

I am confident God will help us in our spiritual walk as we dig deep into His Word. He will strengthen our knowledge of Him while building our confidence that He can turn things around for our favor and blessing. In Isaiah 41:10 (ESV), God says, "Fear not, for I am with you; be not dismayed, for I am your God; I will strengthen you, I will help you, I will uphold you with my righteous right hand." **Be not dismayed**. Other meanings of the word "dismayed" are utter disheartenment, daunting, sudden loss of courage, and, my favorite, *agitation of the mind*. Our mental health takes a toll too. God not only said to "Fear not," but He included the phrase, "be not dismayed," knowing there will be times when our courage will falter, our hearts will check out, and our minds will be agitated.

We can have the latest gadgets, coolest technology, a detailed planner, but all of the greatest inventions and research won't calm an agitated mind. But God—He can. May we take time today to pause enough to reflect on El Roi, The God Who Sees. Let us take time and ask ourselves if we believe He is able to help us where we are. God went to where the Israelites were and saved them. God pursues us and meets us where we are now. Let's ask for the faith to believe He sees, He knows, and He will work on our behalf and bring rest to our souls. When we think of God, let our spirit rise in hope. Let us find hope in the One who will establish our steps.

May we set our minds on Him in order to pursue our purpose in strength. For some of us, we need to renew how we see God. It takes time to instill strongly rooted beliefs in our spirits and minds. We must be intentional with what we read, practice, and meditate on. Take time to not only read today's scripture but make an extra attempt to repeat key verses which help you know who God is and how He helps us. Whether we are groaning, laughing, crying, or just there, He will meet us. He is #TheGodWhoSeesMe.

POWER POINTS

Exodus 2:24-25
Isaiah 41:10
Hebrews 13:8

POWER MOMENT

Lord, thank you for another day of life. God, may my heart truly believe You see and know what I am facing and dealing with. May I wholeheartedly believe the God I serve is able to fight, protect, and help me no matter where I am. Lord, I ask for supernatural strength during times of frustration and for joy to radiate from within me, regardless of my circumstances. God, whatever hard situation, challenge, or season I am in, may You please move in a mighty way so I can end my day with ease and satisfaction. May I place my trust and hope in The One Who Sees and have great expectations for what You have planned for me. I ask for mental clarity, peace of mind, and protection over my emotional, mental, and physical well-being. God, You are mighty, all-powerful, and faithful. May I think of those attributes when I think of You. In Jesus' name, amen!

SMART GOALS

Select - Choose a verse to meditate on. Write it below.

_____

_____

_____

Marinate - Once you have chosen a verse, let it sink into your spirit. What thoughts or impressions do you feel the Holy Spirit is revealing to you?

_____

_____

_____

Ask- Ask God for clarity and wisdom as you finish up the day's reading. Ask what He would like you to do or improve. Ask Him for help if there is an area of need or a way you can bless someone else in need.

_____

_____

_____

Reveal- What has God revealed to you during this devotional time? Write down any thoughts or revelations.

_____

_____

_____

Take action- What is a practical step you can take after reading today's chapter or selected verse?

_____

_____

_____

#Accountable

"All we have to decide is what to do with the time that is given us."[5]

J.R.R. Tolkien

Only, let each one live the life which the Lord has assigned him, and to which God has called him [for each person is unique and is accountable for his choices and conduct, let him walk in this way].
1 Corinthians 7:17, AMP

We are accountable.

Several things come to mind when I read this verse, but I will start with accountability. As every teacher knows, districts use data and performance benchmarks, plus local and state testing to gauge the progress of students and school systems. I will be the first to say I am not against monitoring progress. I actually see the benefits of making sure we track and focus on each student, monitoring their growth (hold the eye rolls; keep reading). The problem with today's testing methods is the overuse of standardized assessments with minimal regard to other forms of progress monitoring. All of these tests create piles of paperwork which sometimes give little insight as to which direction to go. I have had more than my share of tests provide me absolutely no feedback I can use for instruction. In the educational arena, we often get stuck on 'more is better,' and in regards to testing, it's actually the furthest from the truth. As teachers, we know progress is monitored by knowing our goals and tracking how the student is advancing as a whole person. Where did they start? Did they make gains? What factors could be hindering them from attaining the goal we set in place?

Now, let me ask you some questions. What if a teacher didn't know what the goals or standards were for their subject or grade level? Would they be able to accurately assess if a student was proficient, advanced, or in need of extra intervention? How could a teacher navigate their lesson planning and activities if they didn't know their ultimate goal? Have you ever met a teacher who seemed lost and clueless on what the focus was? Does not knowing objectives make a difference in the quality of instruction?

Honestly, one reason I don't like switching grade levels is my lack of comfort and confidence in what is expected from the grade. Anytime we switch from one level to the next, it takes effort and commitment to truly know what the standards are to be able to efficiently plan, guide, and instruct with excellence. My hat's off to all my fellow teacher friends who constantly switch grade levels, subjects, or (heaven forbid) do combination classes! My homeschooling parents, wow, this takes great intentionality. You go, mighty multitasker! However, just as we must know standards and purpose in our profession, we, as Christians, have goals and purposes in our daily life. When we are grounded in truth and purpose, it helps us keep our aim steady and our focus intact. So, the question today is: Do you know your purpose? Do you know what your goal is right now in life? Let me encourage you to stop and look at 1 Corinthians 7:17 one more time (I will wait).

In the verse above, the apostle Paul gives us a great reminder: We will be held accountable for our actions and choices, not just when we are being watched, but every moment of our lives. Knowing what we are held accountable for helps us self-monitor and regulate our steps. Paul states, "Let each one live the life which the Lord has assigned him, and to which God has called him" (1 Corinthians 7:17, ESV). Friend, if you are reading this devotional, I am assuming you are in the educational system in some manner. Whether in the public, private, or homeschooling sector of education, it is where God has assigned you. You may not like it right now. Your eyes may be wandering to do something else, but right now, this is where you have been placed. Regardless of how you got here, you are here. With this in mind, I will encourage and remind you, God has you right where He wants you for this season in your life.

We will be held accountable for our choices, actions, and representation of Him. There has never been a time like now where focused, passionate, and purpose-driven teachers are needed across the nation. God has placed us in this time to be the frontrunners for change, excellence, and hope to a generation who may be struggling with more than just academic issues. We have the opportunity to be voices of reason and justice for the direction in which education is headed. When we speak up with Godly wisdom, we create positive ripples of change for those who come after us. The work we are doing now is not only an investment in the lives of those we encounter but also an investment in ourselves. Let me explain.

Let's look at the parable of the talents. Matthew 25:14-30 gives a description of a nobleman who went away on a business trip and left his servants with different amounts of silver according to their abilities. You can read it yourself for clarity, but to summarize, the story states one servant received five bags of silver, another two bags, and the last received one bag of silver. The parable describes what each servant did with what they were given. When the nobleman returned from his trip, he asked for an account of what each servant was entrusted with. The one with five bags of silver invested the funds and earned five more bags. The servant who had two bags also put the money to work and got two more bags of silver. Now, here's where the story gets awkward. The last servant with one bag of silver allowed fear, distorted perspective, and lack of purpose to cause him to do nothing with what was entrusted to him. Here's the clue: He had no idea what his purpose was. When each servant was asked to give an account for their bags of silver, both the one with five bags and two bags responded, "Master, you gave me five (or two) bags of silver to **invest**…" (NLV, emphasis added). Did you catch that? Do you see how both servants knew what the purpose was for the money given to them? They had the focus and aim to invest. They knew what was expected from them, to **invest**.

On the contrary, we see the third servant who was given one bag of silver respond, "Master, I knew you were a harsh man, harvesting crops you didn't plant and gathering crops you didn't cultivate. I was afraid I would lose your money, so I hid it in the earth. Look, here is your money back" (NLT). There seems to be a disconnect between what the first two servants understood, and what the third servant misconceived. The first two servants showed a clear understanding of what was expected from them. They were entrusted with coins to make a profit and bring a surplus where they were. We don't know how they made a profit, but we know they invested and got to work. Because they knew their purpose, it positioned them to be intentional with their choices and what they did with their funds.

The third servant was stuck on his views that the nobleman was "harsh" and allowed fear, complacency, and uncertainty to keep him from doing his best with what he was given. Friends, we were not given bags of coins, but we were given a position in life. We were given the opportunity and ability to teach and meet the needs of those entrusted in our care. Some of us may have more than others. Some of us may feel like what we've been given isn't as 'good' or 'enough' compared to someone else, but that's not our battle to fight. What we can do is do our best with what we have and invest in it to yield a greater return. Each day we wake up and pray before work, we are investing in the lives present in our sphere of influence. When we give our best, even though it may go unnoticed, we are sowing the seeds of faithfulness and integrity. Every time we decide to be a good steward of our time and intentionally plan to meet the needs of our students, we are investing. We keep ourselves #accountable when we focus on multiplying what God has given us. We cannot cultivate learning, growing, and a harvest of bright learners if we are not planting the best we have. I see myself in the same manner as the servants. I was given a position in life to do good with the talents the Lord has given me. I will not waste time focusing on what others have, my own negative feelings, or frequent disheartenment. Maybe the third servant was spot on with his perception and understanding of the master, but it didn't justify his lack of work and stewardship. Either way, he was still entrusted with something to do. And either way, he was held #accountable. We may also find ourselves in a lackluster predicament, feeling like just taking what we have and doing the minimum. But friend, let's instead take the challenge to see past the moment and our struggles and onward to our higher calling, our greater purpose. Let us do our best with what we have and believe God for the outcome and reward.

As we know from our own upbringing, background, and experience, we don't all start from the same playing field. We may not have the same 'talents' someone else possesses, but we are each given an opportunity. Let's not waste the skill, time, and chance given to us by being idle, complacent, complaining, or bitter. I may not be known as the best or even be the best at what I do, but I will give my best and pray for God to bless the work of my hands. I want to know at the end of the quarter, semester, school year, or at any time at all, that I gave back what was given to me. I want to make sure I am fully aware of my purpose, not to just occupy space, but to matter.

Friends, to those we teach, we matter. Whether they appreciate it now or not, we will do our best for our audience of one, God. Take time to think about your role, your position, and focus on His purpose for us to invest what we have. The servants who invested did so with an understanding of what was expected of them, without knowing the master would come back. Let us trust God sees our investment and will multiply our return in ways we can't even imagine, bearing in mind, the reward may not always be what we physically see but often what changes internally.

POWER POINTS

1 Corinthians 7:17
Matthew 25:14-30

POWER MOMENT

God, my purpose is anchored in You. May You help me to not just know my purpose but live it each and every day. May I be highly favored and blessed as I carry out Your will in my life. Jesus, help me be a good steward of what You have entrusted to me. If I have been complacent or idle, not making the best use of my time, please forgive me. Help me be effective and powerful in my teaching, guiding, and planning that I will be known for my efficiency because of Your power in me. God, thank You for my calling. Thank You for the purpose You have given me. May I remember I am victorious, more than a conqueror, and believe You will reward those who are faithful with their calling. In Jesus' name, amen.

SMART GOALS

Select - Choose a verse to meditate on. Write it below.

_____

_____

_____

Marinate - Once you have chosen a verse, let it sink into your spirit. What thoughts or impressions do you feel the Holy Spirit is revealing to you?

_____

_____

_____

Ask- Ask God for clarity and wisdom as you finish up the day's reading. Ask what He would like you to do or improve. Ask Him for help if there is an area of need or a way you can bless someone else in need.

_____

_____

_____

Reveal- What has God revealed to you during this devotional time? Write down any thoughts or revelations.

_____

_____

_____

Take action- What is a practical step you can take after reading today's chapter or selected verse?

_____

_____

_____

#MissionField

"A calling from God is a calling from God no matter what perks are attached to it."[6]

Michelle Meyers

A calling from God can easily be overlooked when we are too busy admiring others. Our calling can seem so minuscule when using the wrong measuring tools for 'success'. We can easily get tangled up in distractions which cause us to overlook what God has us doing right now.

What is a calling from God? How do we ensure we are doing what He wants? The Word tells us God has called us to love Him with all our heart, soul, and mind and to love our neighbor as ourselves (Mark 12:30-31). Just by reading this devotional, you demonstrate a heart to seek God and grow in Him. He has called us to share His good news and make His name known (Psalm 105:1). We have a mission field right in front of us every day. With our actions, words, and conduct, we can share the gospel of a loving Savior. It is through how we connect with those around us that we can fulfill His calling in our lives.

Teaching is a significant calling from God. I haven't always viewed it as so. Many times, I felt as though ministry work was mainly confined within the walls of the church's physical location. Without meaning to, I had separated my career from my spiritual calling. I compartmentalized serving the Lord separately from my profession within my own mind because I didn't realize how much my attitude, character, and actions shared the gospel without words. We know we are Christ's "hands and feet;" more specifically, 1 Corinthians 12:27 (NLT) acknowledges, "All of you together are Christ's body, and each of you is a part of it." Each of us plays a part in the work of the Lord by sharing His love, His heart of service, and His ability to bring wisdom, guidance, and encouragement to others. Jesus himself was a teacher showing others the way to live life abundantly. He always took this role as a teacher with high regard. Whether teaching one person or huge crowds, He did so with great intentionality and excellence. Jesus came to bring us life and to teach us how to live.

I know we work in a profession which isn't as appreciated as it should be. But, can I mention Jesus wasn't appreciated much either during His time here on earth? Actually, He did many great works and wonders, and people still refused to acknowledge or appreciate what He did or who He was. I think about this when I start to get discouraged by my calling as a teacher. I ponder the significance of our contributions in life and what matters most. I think about Jesus giving His all until the very end, and I wonder how? How did He love, lead, teach, inspire, and give His best when everyone around Him took and took and hardly ever gave back?

Purpose. That's how.

Jesus knew what He was doing was more than the temporal or physical status of what others perceived. He understood He was bringing life, truth, and hope to a world lost and fallen. His purpose was higher than receiving an earthly reward of affirmation, which feels good at the moment, but won't carry to the finish line. His purpose pushed Him forward even when He felt too weary to continue (Luke 22:42). His purpose and the knowledge that what He was doing was fulfilling a plan ordained by God kept Him focused. Hebrews 12:2 (NIV) reflects on what gave Jesus perseverance. "For the joy set before him, he endured the cross, scorning its shame, and sat down at the right hand of the throne of God." You may wonder how this verse plays a role in what we deal with as educators. Let's continue to verse three, "Consider him who endured such opposition from sinners, so that you will not grow weary and lose heart." **Don't. Lose. Heart.** Let's just make it clear right up front, we won't always feel like giving our best. There will be days, maybe even weeks, when we feel detached from our love of teaching or even question if we 'love' what we do. But when we think of our purpose, our why, we can get a firmer grip on life and continue forward. No matter where we are teaching, we have committed to serving those entrusted to us each year.

Here's a familiar scenario: We are given curriculum (hopefully), standards, guidelines, and goals to meet for the year. We aim to get our students proficient in all academic areas; we hope they love coming to school and are motivated to learn. We get our classes ready, start planning our beginning of the year activities, get excited for all the wonderful new things we want to implement and try. We even invest in the fancy planner all decked out with stickers and colored pens. I mean, We. Are. Ready.

And then it happens. Reality sets in. This job isn't for the faint of heart. There are challenges: not enough time, never feeling prepared, and just as fast as we felt ready to start, we are now ready to finish. We may even be tempted with thoughts to just do the bare minimum or even harbor bitterness and anger over too many behavioral issues or lack of support. These may be justifiable reasons to be upset and frustrated, but they are not worthy enough to steal our joy and purpose. We have a calling to live as Jesus did. He knew His calling. Even through pain, weariness, and brutal circumstances, He found His purpose greater than the temporary discomfort. We will experience our own discomforts during the school year, but remember your goals and His purpose when you started.

When my mental fortitude and spirit are being challenged, and I can tell #teachertired struggles are kicking in high gear, I speak to myself. I remind my spirit of who I am in Christ, and how He desires I live. I try to rehearse these affirmations in my mind, in hopes that my heart will get a pump of faith fuel to fill my empty cup.

I will remember what I do now impacts future lives.
I will give my best, even though I don't feel like it, I don't think it's worth it, I think it's too hard for me, (you fill in the blank).
I will bring glory to God by leading with excellence.
I will feed my spirit with wisdom, knowledge, and support through the Word of God.
I will give God my feelings and have faith He will provide the energy needed to carry out the purpose He has called me to this year.
I will give this battle to the Lord and remember He fights for me.

These are some of my 'course-correct' thoughts I have used. What thoughts can you speak over yourself to help you redirect yourself from #teachertired to teaching in truth? Our mindset really does affect our whole being. Remember, feelings do not dictate truth. They can help us sense when there is a need, disconnect, or struggle, but they make terrible life compasses. Even when our feelings dictate otherwise, I encourage you to stand on God's truth for guidance.

Exodus 14:14 (NIV) reminds us, "The LORD will fight for you; you need only to be still." Some translations say, "just stay calm." We need calmness during hectic times. We need to know what we have been called to do is so very important. Do not let the enemy fixate your mind on what's too hard for you and make you forget who fights for you and gives you victory.

Keep your purpose and why intact. We may not have a million-dollar platform with a spotlight directed on us, but we have been given a unique opportunity to connect with people we probably never would have met on our own. Let's be honest, if you're anything like me, you tend to keep to your own circle of friends. We are drawn to hang out with those who share similar interests and traits, yet if we only live life with those who are the same, how do we share God's love with those who aren't? How do we reach others for Christ and show love by keeping to ourselves? As teachers, we have been given a window of opportunity each year to come in contact with new students, new parents, and a new chance to share the good news while equipping students for the 21st century.

We are called to share the good news. We do this each day we show up to our #missionfield, a.k.a. the classroom and our workplace. We share the good news when we take time to help others, listen to a co-worker who may be struggling, help out another teacher who is in need, or even help a short-staffed cafeteria with a good attitude (you know it happens!). We share the good news of Christ's love by showing up with our best effort and giving focused attention to students who may not get any encouragement or validation otherwise. Unlike most other professions, what we do on a daily basis can literally speak life or death into a person's soul.

I don't know about you, but I can specifically remember certain teachers who made me stand a little taller, sing a little louder, and have the courage to try, all because they believed in me. I remember my fifth-grade teacher heard me sing "My Country 'Tis of Thee" after our morning pledge, as was the routine back in the days. She leaned over and whispered to me, "Gina, you have such a beautiful voice." People, you should have seen the smile on my face and heard how much louder I sang that morning all because someone took the time to speak life into a girl's spirit. And let me tell you, I was a very insecure and hurting little girl. My teacher didn't know what I was dealing with at home, but that moment filled my bucket more than words can describe. All these years later, I still remember that one small moment in time. It makes me more aware of the power and influence we have been given as educators.

Our purpose is real. Our purpose is needed. Our purpose exceeds the platform we have. Don't for one minute let the enemy lie to you and minimize what you are doing. We may not see the harvest or fruit right away, but God is our reward and will satisfy us with good things. Psalms 103:5 (NIV) reveals He is the one "who satisfies your desires with good things so that your youth is renewed like the eagle's." Satisfies our desires with good things... youth is renewed... yes, I will take a sip on those refreshing words! Hear me, friends. Even when the world doesn't seem to compensate us fairly, God will. It may be in forms of mental ease, joy in our spirit, renewed perspective, contentment, and yes, even financial provision. The key is to trust and believe what His Word says. We are His hands and feet at our workplace. We are doing more than teaching standards and objectives; we are sharing the love God has placed inside of us to anyone we meet along the way. Our #missionfield is right where God has placed us.

I once had a student who struggled with learning so much it was actually causing marital problems between his parents. After our first parent-teacher conference and witnessing his dad's negative criticism of his mom's parenting style, I could see their child's 'subpar' grades were causing a rift between the parents and with the child. The mom would come to class looking so hopeless and so frustrated, all she could express was anger or short temperedness with her child.

Now, you may think we have no place in helping. We are not trained marriage counselors. And you are correct, we are not marriage counselors, but we do have a hand in helping families. I realized from this encounter that I was placed in this young man's life for more than just helping him meet grade-level expectations. I was placed in his life to speak truth, encouragement, and hope to a boy who was headed down a path of low self-worth and lost identity. I, a first-grade teacher, was given an opportunity to come in and battle the lies of the enemy over this boy and bring confidence, courage, and hope. I, a schoolteacher, was given the chance to close poked holes in this boy's heart and give him the confidence to believe and dream of a bright future. I was given only nine months to sow seeds of hope and love and pray God would water his soul along the way.

The other chance I had to help was to share the vision of who this boy was with his mom. I made sure to encourage her and tell her of his potential; of how he is capable of doing so much. Was his progress slow? Yes. But was he actually trying and showing more confidence? Yes! Progress is progress no matter how small. I became more intentional with my words when speaking to his mom. I aimed to encourage her and give her ideas on how to help him. I reminded her she was not 'wasting' time, even if she did not see the gains she desired fast enough. It's crazy how the Holy Spirit will lead you to what others need when you include Him in all you do. When I told the mom those simple words, I saw her eyes water and could tell something struck a chord deep inside of her.

I share this experience to encourage you to ask God to open the eyes of your heart to where He is needing you to step in. We cannot limit our purpose and calling to a contract. Trust me. God has His hand on you and each family you encounter. We don't have to preach Bible verses to each person to show God's character. We show God's character every time we are intentional with our words, time, and effort. Jesus gave His best and so should we.

You have been given unique traits and gifts others need. God has placed those exact students in your path for a reason. Each day you believe and embrace your workplace calling; you become one day closer to helping a young child or adult understand their calling. You were called into this profession for such a time as this. You are needed. Be the change you want to see.

POWER POINTS

Mark 12:30-31
Psalm 105:1
1 Corinthians 12:27
Luke 22:42
Hebrew 12:2
Exodus 14:14
Psalm 103:5

POWER MOMENT

Jesus, thank You so much for the position You have given me in life. Thank You that no matter what the enemy could possibly do to distract, harm, or hurt me, You, Lord, work all things for good for those who love You. Lord, I love You. I need You. Help me to not forget my job as an educator runs deeper than a pacing guide, checked off standards, or curriculum. You have given me Your Holy Spirit to make an impact and touch the hearts and minds of learners, parents, and those I meet. I need You to direct me; help me be grounded in who You created me to be, so I may live with excellence in all I do. Take my classroom, the students I teach, my colleagues, and the administration I work under and bless me with supernatural favor, strength, and focus. Lord, may those around me know and see the Lord is with me. God, thank You for this calling on my life; I depend on Your grace and wisdom to carry me and lead me each day. If there is anyone in need of encouragement or hope, I speak life and times of refreshing over them in Jesus' name. Lord, you are real. My needs and desires are real. Please hear and answer me. May I live a purpose-driven life! In Jesus' name, amen.

SMART GOALS

Select - Choose a verse to meditate on. Write it below.

_____

_____

_____

Marinate - Once you have chosen a verse, let it sink into your spirit. What thoughts or impressions do you feel the Holy Spirit is revealing to you?

_____

_____

_____

Ask- Ask God for clarity and wisdom as you finish up the day's reading. Ask what He would like you to do or improve. Ask Him for help if there is an area of need or a way you can bless someone else in need.

_____

_____

_____

Reveal- What has God revealed to you during this devotional time? Write down any thoughts or revelations.

_____

_____

_____

Take action- What is a practical step you can take after reading today's chapter or selected verse?

_____

_____

_____

#ThePowerofaPrayingTeacher

"Relying on God has to begin all over again every day as if nothing had yet been done."[7]

C.S. Lewis

It was a new school year. A new beginning and hopefully a fresh start from the dreaded year which almost took me out of teaching altogether. This year though, I was more aware of my need to pray for the 'best fit' class. Meaning, I asked God to place students in my class who would work well with me and I with them. This was the year I was moved more than ever to make sure I prayed for parents I would encounter, and I prayed for the extra support my heart yearned for. You best believe I was asking God for favor, favor, favor! However, what He did for me that year set the stage for His sovereignty and glory to be seen. It was a time when my heart started to trust God to take care of me, even outside of my own narrow expectations.

They came rushing in with excitement as most kids do at the start of a new school year. I can't personally vouch for the excitement in middle or high schoolers, but I can say there seems to be a sense of excitement and novelty starting off a new year regardless of grade. My class was vibrant, sweet, and of course ready to learn. It was the first week of school, so you know behavior was pretty on point and smooth (or maybe they were still half asleep from the summer haze). However, the novelty wanes as students become more familiar with their surroundings, true personalities start to emerge. As I navigated through the hustle of the beginning of the school year, trying to make sure I wasn't forgetting deadlines, making sure kids were sent home on the correct bus, trying to keep up to date with my copies and plans, I started to find my mind sinking back into anxious overload. But then it happened, early in the school year, right when my anxiety started to hit, she came into my room.

A parent of one of my students came in after school and asked if she could help out inside the classroom and volunteer. For some of you reading this you may think that's great. You may think, *oh yay! God sent a parent helper.* You may actually wish you had parents asking to help. At this particular season in my life, however, I wanted nothing to do with being too close to parents. I wanted to keep a friendly distance because I was afraid of judgment. I had experienced the sting of parents talking about me. I didn't want to have a parent inside the classroom possibly judging what I was doing. I let fear and worry blind me from seeing a helping hand. I let negative thoughts build up a wall of defense, and I kindly said, "Sure," while everything in me was shrinking back with dread. *Ugh, what if she doesn't like how I manage the class? What if she's a distraction to her child? What will I have her do? God, I don't want her help in the classroom; it's just uncomfortable.* All of these thoughts and more came rushing in my mind. Looking back now, I can see they all stemmed from fear, insecurity, and just straight up stinkin' thinkin'. I remember asking God to help me with confidence when she would come in and make sure our class wasn't crazy, so I wouldn't lose control or seem incompetent (sounds crazy as I write all of this out, but I seriously suffered panic when parents came in). I just couldn't afford to leave anything to chance, even having parents come into the classroom was covered in prayers, too! I don't always go to prayer first as I should, but I am learning it is my biggest ally.

The first day she came in to help, I had picked a time when the kiddos were at electives to help me get to know her better. I mean, c'mon guys, if you're anything like me and feel the 'feels' of having parents in the classroom, I had to start off having her come when no kids were around. I was easing into this slowly. (I am literally laughing at myself as I write this, because am I the only odd one like this? Possibly…).

After a couple of moments of her cutting some lamination for me, she said, "I am praying for you and the class…my daughter truly enjoys being in your classroom." As soon as those words came out, it was as if a crack was made in the defensive wall I had built up. I could sense there was a jump in my spirit, a hard to explain joy to meet someone else who was a believer. To actually have a parent who cared enough to pray for me, and our class, was God sent, I knew it. She was a parent I knew I wanted and needed.

Friends, I didn't take this blessing lightly because I knew what kind of year I had just barely survived. I knew if there was any way I was going to make it in this profession, it would be dependent on the grace of God. And what God did was send me a prayer warrior to fight alongside me. He sent me a praying parent. He sent me someone who I knew was for me and not against me. He sent someone as a reminder to me that He had not forgotten me. He showed me He had heard my prayers for support and encouragement. Throughout the school year, she came in and saw challenges and prayed on her own for students. She prayed for me and encouraged me in a manner God knew I needed in this season. I was a teacher with a fragile heart. I was a teacher who was wounded from the strenuous side of teaching. I needed help and my hope restored. Oh, what a gift of finding prayer partners. She was a gift to me.

Maybe right now you can think of parents who have been supportive to you. Maybe you can think of an instance when God sent someone as a support system to encourage you on occasion or throughout the school year. If so, do not dismiss it as a coincidence. God can and will provide us with support. I pray our eyes would be open to those people, resources, or opportunities sent by His grace. I pray our eyes would be open because when that parent first offered to help me, I was not open to it. I wanted to be on my own, figure things out, and keep a distance from people. Sometimes, we can be so self-consumed with our concerns, or our past pains, we don't realize when there is a helping hand in front of us. We want help, but fail to see it.

On the flip side, maybe you are thinking you've never had this type of support. Maybe you work in a school setting where there is no parental involvement and having parents offer to come in to help is foreign. Maybe you are teaching solo in your home and do not have a connection with others. May I suggest we pray for divine intervention? May I suggest we pray for support and help? May I propose we be open to help coming in forms other than parents or our own constructed solution? I don't ever want to limit God on what or how He will show up for us. I want to be open to believing for change and breakthrough in any form He deems best.

I am also fully aware that some of you reading this now may actually **be the answer** to someone else around you who is in need of a prayer partner or help. Nowadays the whole concept of prayer can get thrown around lightly. We can say, "I will pray for you," but never really pause long enough to do it. Or sometimes, we can even think our situation requires more than 'just prayers.' I am able to write those words because I have felt them at times. Sometimes the reason we do not go straight to prayer is because we lack a true understanding of the power associated with prayer or the true impact it can make on any situation. James 5:16b-18 (NLT) confirms:

> *The earnest prayer of a righteous person has great power and produces wonderful results. Elijah was as human as we are, and yet, when he prayed earnestly for no rain to fall, none fell for three and a half years! Then, when he prayed again, the sky sent down rain and the earth began to yield its crops.*

Let's slow down, pause, and read that again (I will wait for you).

There is so much insight in those verses, and I don't want you or myself to miss it. First, it mentions the earnest prayer of a righteous man. For me, the thought of being a righteous man/ woman is hard to accept because I know my heart and issues. I seem to get stuck on the fact that I don't always feel very righteous or act as such. However, Romans 3:22 (NLT, emphasis added) teaches us that "We are made right with God by placing our faith in Jesus Christ. And this is true for everyone who believes, **no matter who we are**." We are made righteous through our faith in Jesus. Period. It is done. We do not need to work for His approval. We do not need to go to theology school or be ordained by a pastor to be heard by God. No matter who we are, He hears us. When I let self-doubt and condemnation come in my mind, it can be a hindrance to my prayer life and hard to believe God will answer me. First, we must realize we are the righteous person who prays. We must step into God's throne room with the confidence He will hear us. The author of Hebrews further explains because of Christ and our faith in him, we can now come boldly and confidently into God's presence (Hebrews 4:16). We must believe we are righteous through Him and can confidently go to God our Father for any need. If we do not know where we stand with God, we will never feel worthy to ask Him for help, nor will we truly believe He will answer.

Now that we understand our righteousness, let's continue unpacking James 5:16b (NLT, emphasis added). We see that "The **earnest prayer** of a righteous person has **great power** and **produces wonderful results**." 'Earnest' implies having a purpose, being determined, and eager to sincerely pursue something. When we earnestly pray, it is not an, "Oh yeah, I will pray about it," and then totally forget. No, it is an intentional mind-heart-and-soul-unite-and-cry-out-to-the-Lord-for-answers-and-help kind of prayer. Notice I am not making this into a legalistic twelve-step type of prayer plan. Meaning, nowhere does it say we have to be on our knees, or stand in a certain position, or say a certain phrase. It just means you go to God with sincerity and pray. I think the problem

I was facing, and still do at times, is getting too busy to calm my mind. I get so frustrated that prayer doesn't seem to be enough in the moment. Sometimes I actively pursue my anger, fatigue, and frustration in venting to coworkers and my husband rather than seeing prayer as the ultimate outlet for change. Venting to friends isn't wrong (unless we go overboard and say things we shouldn't; that mouth of ours can lead us into trouble y'all!), but when complaining takes the wheel and has more of a spotlight than our prayer life, then maybe we need a heart check.

So, let's keep this in mind when we think about earnest prayers; let's be intentional. This may look different for each person. Maybe for some, we like to have a prayer journal to help us keep focused. Maybe for others, it's more of a list of things we need to be reminded to pray for. Maybe for some, it's setting an actual time and scheduling it so that we definitely stop and pray. For me, I know I can pray as I drive to work, but I also know I need a separate time of prayer because I can get distracted when I am trying to pray and do other things; that's just me. We know life is complicated, with constant ups and downs; therefore, let us grow in our prayer life continually. The best fight against any attack or challenge is prayer. It is also a great way to give God thanks and acknowledgment for who He is and what He has done. Our prayer time is between us and God, and that, my dear friends, is what makes it so special. We just need to remember prayer can happen anywhere and at any moment. It is a constant open communication between us and the Lord. Prayer can happen when our class has decided to go haywire and we want to blow up. Prayer can help us keep our mouths shut when we want to say something out of anger. We can ask God at any moment for calmness, ease, and supernatural self-control. Yes, God is our ever-present help in our time of need. He's also readily available to praise when we see and acknowledge how good He has been to us. Prayer is our means to change and the medium by which we grow closer to our heavenly Father.

Now, let us look at what happens when believers pray. The Word says the prayer of a righteous person has "great power and produces wonderful results" (James 5:16, NLT). That right there should give you a sense of empowerment. A straighten-up-your-back-a-little-and-lift-your-head kind of feeling. We need to start believing we are not fighting a losing battle. We can't be when God is on our side and has already claimed the victory! I didn't say it wasn't a hard, difficult, or sometimes daunting battle, but there is power for change and victory in Jesus' name! When we want change, power, and wonderful results, we start with prayer. Friends, let us be praying teachers who take our students, parents, administration, lessons, thoughts…*errrythang* to the Lord!

I've had people look down on me for saying, "I will pray about it." I have had people in my family tell me there's more to do than *just* pray. What they do not understand is prayer is not the end, but the *beginning*. It opens up the pathway for communication between us and God. Prayer sets us up to receive wisdom and insight on what to do, what actions to take. Prayer is an action step.

If we go blindly into planning, teaching, collaborating, and trying to deal with defiant behavior on our own strength, we are destined to fail because we are human. What we do in our jobs requires more than human strength. We need supernatural strength, wisdom, and favor. Let's be real here, our profession is hard, and filled with so much pressure we need God's abundant help. I believe it starts with prayer and a heart that believes for wonderful results. Why? Because He said so.

As we read further in the passage, James gives reference to the prophet Elijah stating, "Elijah was as **human as we are**, and yet when he prayed earnestly that no rain would fall, none fell for three and a half years" (James 5:17 NLT emphasis added). I love this because it confirms God didn't just answer Elijah's prayer because he was famous or a well-known prophet. No, he was human as we are, meaning, he had his own issues. He dealt with fear, anger, frustration, and disappointments along the way. He wasn't perfect or loved more by God than us. *He was human just as we are.* I will note: it's pretty stinkin' cool how he prayed for no rain and God answered him. I mean, talk about a big, bold prayer! But what's really neat about this is the same God who answered Elijah still listens to us today. No matter how big or small our need, there is nothing He can't do. He hears us when we ask Him to help calm the atmosphere in our classroom. He hears us when we ask for wisdom on how to engage or plan for our students. He hears us when we are faced with challenges which make us want to quit our jobs. If He can make it rain for one person, I am sure He can shower us with blessings, favor, and breakthrough.

Lastly, let us remember this classic verse, yet a verse I always seem to have to remind myself of: "You do not have because you do not ask God" (James 4:2b NIV). This verse goes on to remind us we should ask for things with pure intentions, according to His purpose. However, the point I am trying to make clear is as teachers, we need to step up our prayer life and remember what power we have in prayer. We can include God even in the mundane everyday tasks we face and give them to the Lord. Invite Him to add fuel to our fire and pour into our empty cups by making prayer a priority. Let us become teachers who pray. Better yet, what if we unite with other fellow teachers and pray? What if God is prompting you to start up a prayer group with other teachers at work? What if, even just once a month, we believers gathered and prayed over classes, students, administration, and the well-being of teachers? What if we united and covered the never-ending demands of our profession with prayer? The possibilities are endless. #ThePowerofaPrayingTeacher is real and produces wonderful results.

I want to leave you with this quote from evangelist Billy Graham: "True prayer is a way of life, not just for use in cases of emergency. Make it a habit, and when the need arises you will be in practice."[8] We don't have to be perfect to be prayer warriors. He promises us that when we draw near to Him, He will draw near to us (James 4:8 NIV). With God by our side, we can hope and expect greater days. May we unleash the power we have as praying teachers!

POWER POINTS

James 5:16b- 18
James 4:2b
James 4:8
Romans 3:22
Hebrews 4:16

POWER MOMENT

God, you know exactly where I am. You know the need, the concern, and every frustration. Jesus, sometimes I find it hard to pause and pray. Sometimes God, I honestly may not feel like it. But, Lord, I ask right now for You to quicken me through Your Holy Spirit to be intentional in my prayer life. Help me not get consumed with complaining, bickering, or murmuring, allowing the enemy to plant discord or bitterness in my heart. Lord, I can't change others, but I can change myself and my outlook on things. God, I believe prayer changes things. I believe there is power in Your word. Numbers 23:19 (NLV) confirms, you are not a man, that you should lie; what You say, You will do! Therefore, please hear my earnest prayers and let there be a breakthrough in every area of concern. Lord, if there are behavioral issues in my classroom, please settle them. If there is a need for encouragement and help, I pray for divine intervention. Help me with my mental, emotional, and physical well-being so I can be effective and bless those around me. God, help me be a powerfully praying teacher who seeks Your face. Lord, I wait and expect wonderful results, just as James 5:16b promises. I believe because You are my wonderful and faithful God. I love you, Father; thank you for helping me, in Jesus' name, amen!

SMART GOALS

Select - Choose a verse to meditate on. Write it below.

_____

_____

_____

Marinate - Once you have chosen a verse, let it sink into your spirit. What thoughts or impressions do you feel the Holy Spirit is revealing to you?

_____

_____

_____

Ask- Ask God for clarity and wisdom as you finish up the day's reading. Ask what He would like you to do or improve. Ask Him for help if there is an area of need or a way you can bless someone else in need.

_____

_____

_____

Reveal- What has God revealed to you during this devotional time? Write down any thoughts or revelations.

_____

_____

_____

Take action- What is a practical step you can take after reading today's chapter or selected verse?

_____

_____

_____

#UnityinDiversity

"None of us are as smart as all of us."[9]

Kenneth H. Blanchard

I vividly remember listening to one of my favorite speakers Ravi Zacharias[10] describe how higher institutional places of learning coined the term 'university.' He mentioned how diverse thinking, diverse experiences, and diverse backgrounds work together to form a sense of unity in diversity, which led to the term *university* which represents our higher education system. No two students will be the same. Progress will look different for each individual, and the methods in which we engage to disperse information will vary depending on the unique characteristics of each person. Diversity is just a glimpse of God's uniqueness. Let us embrace differences rather than uniform them. Whether in the public, private, or homeschooling sector of learning and development, diversity needs to be recognized and appreciated.

This concept is true for those who collaborate in the educational field. We all come to the table with different backgrounds, different personalities, different states, different mindsets, and various student teaching experiences. Basically, we're all just downright different! With this diversity amongst educators, it can be a challenge to form cohesive teams who have common ground. However, as a believer in the teaching field, we have a superpower which combats any form of discord, isolation, or tendency to gossip. We have the spirit of peace and understanding who lives inside of us. We may not be able to control who we work with, but we can control our thoughts, actions, and attitude.

I know firsthand what it's like to be in a grade level with turbulence. Meetings can be toxic and draining. There can be more time spent debating than actually working together. There are times when just the thought of 'team planning' can make us cringe or sick to the stomach. I get it, I've been there. (If you have never felt this way and don't know what I am talking about, I am glad, because seriously, it's no fun.) However, tension and turmoil do not have to be the norm or constant atmosphere, especially when we believers are present.

First, I will admit I have not always been the best team player. Looking back, I am sure I could have spoken up more, maybe even spoken less behind closed doors (yes, I am calling myself out). I am not perfect or claim to be the master of collaboration, but I can say, God's word does have insight on how to interact, on the importance of teamwork and cohesiveness. Ecclesiastes 4:9-10 (NIV) reminds us, "Two are better than one, because they have a good return for their labor: If either of them falls down, one can help the other up. But pity anyone who falls and has no one to help them up."

Our colleagues are not opponents, enemies, or distant individuals in neighboring classrooms. We are not called to do life alone, and we are definitely not called to be educators living inside our own bubble, no matter how much we love our personal space. "Two are better than one, *because* they have a good return for their labor." In our field, we need to learn to work smarter not harder. We need as much unity and support as we can get. The systematic approach to increasing professional learning communities in our schools and work environments is actually a powerful notion. We know there is purpose in collaboration and great reward when done effectively. Problems arise when it is not done efficiently or when we feel like it is a waste of our time.

What can cause so much tension and stress within collaboration? One big hurdle can be our different perspectives, attitudes, and temperaments. The same diversity which is woven into the university framework can also be a stumbling block for many individuals. We can come off as harsh, rude, or indifferent. Maybe we feel as though others are hard to deal with and we shut down. Maybe we deal with insecure thoughts, thinking what we have to say isn't 'good enough' or important. Maybe we feel unheard and have chosen to stop participating altogether. These are real feelings that can arise when working with others. However, if there was ever anyone who was the master of collaboration and unity, it was Jesus. Just think about it. He walked alongside twelve disciples, all of whom were different (think: tax collector, fishermen, zealot, tradesmen, business owners) and carried their own emotional and mental baggage. Some disciples had negative outlooks, some doubted Jesus along the way, and a couple even betrayed Him and used Him.

We are called to live as Jesus lived while on earth. As 1 John 2:6 (NLT) proclaims, "Those who say they live in God should live their lives as Jesus did." *"Those who say."* Think about those words. If we are professing Christianity and can talk the talk and call ourselves believers, then our walk and actions need to align with His word and instruction. What instructions are we given? We are directed to live our lives the way Jesus did. Even among a great diverse following, Jesus somehow found a way to bring the most unlikely people together for the single purpose of spreading the Good News. So much so, they were willing to drop everything and follow Him. Am I suggesting we preach the gospel during collaboration time? No, not necessarily with words, but I am suggesting the way we handle discord and promote unity will speak louder than any audible words ever could. Have you heard people talking loudly, but not saying much? My prayer is for God to give us wisdom and clarity to have favor during meetings, insight on how to solve problems, and self-control to stay focused on being productive.

Whatever happens, conduct yourselves in a manner worthy of the gospel of Christ. Then, whether I come and see you or only hear about you in my absence, I will know that you stand firm in the one Spirit, striving together as one for the faith of the gospel.
Philippians 1:27, NIV

So I, the prisoner for the Lord, appeal to you to live a life worthy of the calling to which you have been called [that is, to live a life that exhibits godly character, moral courage, personal integrity, and mature behavior—a life that expresses gratitude to God for your salvation], with all humility [forsaking self-righteousness], and gentleness [maintaining self-control], with patience, bearing with one another in [unselfish] love.
Ephesians 4:1-2, AMP

As I sit here and read over Ephesians 4:2, the following words replay in my heart, "with all humility [forsaking self-righteousness]." It takes tons of humility to not lash out at someone who has offended you or gotten on your last nerve. The Amplified Bible adds the notation "forsaking self-righteousness," meaning we can't always assume we are right, nor should we be condescending in our behaviors. Even if we do have the right to be offended, and have grounds to dispute a matter, *how* we conduct ourselves and *what* we say matters. For the sake of truly internalizing this truth, and just in case any of us forget, we are called to a higher standard. Not always easy, but so very worth it. The higher standard is seen right here in these verses. The scripture continues to instruct us to have "gentleness [maintaining self-control], with patience, bearing with one another in [unselfish] love."

I know. It's a heavy call. It's not for the average heart. These verses are directed to us, men and women of God. We should be light-bearers. We should be leaders in all meetings according to our actions and attitude. It takes a leader, strong and intentional, to be able to do this. Again, I am not saying I have mastered this. I *know* I have failed, but I also thank God for this instruction as a moral compass to get me back on track to how He has called and created me to be.

Personally, I can't say enough how much others have impacted my thinking, teaching, and learning in my career. I have experienced great moments of kindness, acceptance, encouragement, and enlightenment from fellow teachers. I have had unforgettable experiences where people have helped me grow as a whole person. I have also had encounters bring out the worst in me. I have felt anger and resentment when I felt talked about, rejected, or even overlooked. When there is an environment filled with different personalities, experiences, and mindsets, there are bound to be sparks and possible fireworks. Whether good or bad, each feeling, each experience, has important value. How we utilize our past experiences will either make us bitter or better. We decide.

Will there be moments of offense or misunderstanding? Yes. Those factors are part of the territory of having people work together. Collaboration isn't always easy, however, just like we try to teach our own students about working together, we must set the example. It is full of compromise, teamwork, and participation. Shutting down and refusing to participate can be as deadly as spewing out harsh words. Remember, body language is pretty loud, too.

The above verses are key points to help guide us when faced with difficult situations. They remind us to live a life that exhibits Godly character. They remind us we are called to a higher standard. Again, I am not saying it's easy (I feel like I need to keep repeating this). But as believers, what sets us apart is *who* sets us apart. Jesus is the person who sets us apart, to live as He did, in order to be the light in a dark world. We as the light must be stronger in our beliefs, must press past the discomfort and conduct ourselves in a way worthy of His calling. As Matthew 5:15 (NIV) puts it, "Neither do people light a lamp and put it under a bowl. Instead, they put it on its stand, and it gives light to everyone in the house." With this in mind, let us be the light to those we work with and illuminate the places we enter. There can be #UnityinDiversity when we as believers are present. Next time you walk into a meeting or collaboration time, think of these verses and go shine your light like only you can!

POWER POINTS

Ecclesiastes 4:9-11
Philippians 1:27
Ephesians 4:1-2
Matthew 5:15

POWER MOMENT

Lord, I thank You for Your word which is a lamp unto my feet. Thank You for giving me sound Godly wisdom to help me navigate through challenges such as working with those who are different than me. Thank You for strong grade-level teams and please keep them healthy, growing, and effective. God, help those who are currently in situations of challenge and struggle within their teams or with their coworkers. It's hard to feel overlooked or to be worried about saying the wrong thing. It's hard, Lord, to work with a team that is divided. So, I come to You, the God of hope, our God of unity, and ask for help with those I work with. I pray for grade-level teams to become stronger together. I pray where there is offense or hurt feelings for there to be peace and forgiveness. I pray for effectiveness, focus, and elimination of distractions in meetings. God, you said in Your word that "two is better than one," so Lord bring unity as only You can. Help me see how I can change and help. Show me ways I can be a blessing. Help me not murmur and complain but be an answer to the problem. Make me a problem solver. Let there be one accord, good attitudes, and powerful planning, in Jesus' name, amen!

SMART GOALS

Select - Choose a verse to meditate on. Write it below.

_____

_____

_____

Marinate - Once you have chosen a verse, let it sink into your spirit. What thoughts or impressions do you feel the Holy Spirit is revealing to you?

_____

_____

_____

Ask- Ask God for clarity and wisdom as you finish up the day's reading. Ask what He would like you to do or improve. Ask Him for help if there is an area of need or a way you can bless someone else in need.

_____

_____

_____

Reveal- What has God revealed to you during this devotional time? Write down any thoughts or revelations.

_____

_____

_____

Take action- What is a practical step you can take after reading today's chapter or selected verse?

_____

_____

_____

#ToBeTHEONE

"Your beliefs shape your attitudes!"[11]

Andy Stanley

The *one* teacher who is highly requested. The *one* teacher who gets high praise from administration and parents. The *one* teacher who has crazy cool ideas and has parents lining up writing requests to get into their class. You know, *The One Teacher* you must get. The problem with this '*one* teacher' malady is it skews not only what education is about, but it leaves a blurry view on *why* we do what we do. This pressure to be *The One Teacher* places subconscious stress on us to highly perform, to be acknowledged and known for our actions. In subtle ways, it can be a precursor to teacher burnout and feelings of bitterness. It can hinder us from sharing the best, most creative ideas for fear of not getting recognition or standing out amongst the rest. In some crazy way of thinking, we believe if everyone does what we do, we may start to go unnoticed. This perspective can even leave us bitter against the administration if we feel our efforts are down-played, unrecognized, or unvalued.

You may be reading this and have no clue what I am talking about and this is a good thing. But there are many of you who know exactly what I am talking about. Ever have a student in your room, then all of a sudden, a parent requests to have them removed because apparently you weren't '*the one*' they were looking for? (Now, I will interject here and say, sometimes it is needed to have students removed or placed in different environments which benefit both parties; I am not talking about these situations.) Maybe you work your tail off and feel like it never gets recognized, but when teacher so-and-so does something, there's big applause waiting for them. Better yet, have you ever seen or heard about how parents rank teachers? Yeah, all of it can get to you if you're not careful.

To be completely honest with you, aiming to be *'the one'* had actually made its sneaky way into my mind. Early in my teaching years, I found myself desiring to be the educator parents requested. I felt it meant I was doing something right. Somehow, I based my confidence in their approval. I wanted to be *"the one"* teacher who had the high-test scores, great bulletin boards, innovative ideas, and good parent feedback. I had great goals, but the wrong motives. I remember quite well coming up with an idea, only to have another teacher say it was their idea, and I was so bothered I wasn't given credit for it. It sounds silly and kind of embarrassing to admit, but it's true. I wanted the 'shout out,' and I wanted the recognition for coming up with the concept. Now, some of you may think it's normal; we should get credit for our hard work, right? But you see, the Bible mentions us doing our best as unto the Lord. Colossians 3:23-24 (MSG) says, "Work from the heart for your real Master, for God, confident that you'll get paid in full when you come into your inheritance. Keep in mind always that the ultimate Master you're serving is Christ." I will repeat, "Keep in mind *always* that the ultimate Master you're serving is Christ."

Apparently, I did not keep this truth in mind. Without even realizing how it happened, I found myself internally competing with other teachers for approval and recognition. It was an ugly inner battle. This aim to be *'the one'* had slowly opened up a never-satisfied abyss of wanting affirmation, a need to stand out, and a desire to be known as *'the one.'* This black hole of desire is a bottomless pit storing a never-ending feed of negative lies resulting in misplaced focus.

This tension and desire for recognition isn't just found in the teaching arena; it can be seen in any job. It was even seen happening in the Bible. Luke 9:46 (NLT) reads, "Then his disciples began arguing about which of them was the greatest." Now to fully understand this verse, when you have time, read Luke chapter 9, and you will see the apostles were called to do great and mighty works. Jesus had given them all authority and power to drive out demons, cure diseases, proclaim the kingdom of God, and heal the sick (Luke 9:1-2)! I mean, talk about a great career. They had all the power (as do we) to do kingdom work and get going on their mission. During this journey, however, they got into an argument over who would be the greatest. I can't help but find this verse so out of context. Shouldn't they have been singing hymns and praises after witnessing all the miracles with Jesus? Or discussing all of the miracles they had witnessed and what great things they wanted to do next *together*? Talk about an off-topic situation. Just a few verses before, they fed over 5,000 men with five loaves of bread and two fish. The chapter also mentions them going village to village healing the sick proclaiming the Good News. When did they have time to worry or think about who would be the greatest disciple? Why did they even care? But then it hit me. We are human, and in our human mindset, it is easy to let selfish ambition settle into place. If the disciples who physically walked with Jesus dealt with these emotions of wanting to be recognized and noticed, I am sure it is common for it to happen to us some time or another.

Maybe you don't deal with a desire to be recognized, but maybe you volunteer for more than you can handle to show you are involved and hardworking? Maybe the desire to be needed drives your actions. In either case, these motives lead down the same path: one where you are dissatisfied, overworked, and potentially bitter. It never fails when I start to focus on myself and how I am perceived or appreciated, I lose my stamina really quickly. All of a sudden, what God intended to be a blessing in my life becomes more of a burden and heavy weight I want to throw off. I placed this mental and emotional load on myself to please everyone around me. I wanted to make my mark, to prove I was a good teacher, that I was the teacher your child should have. Are you seeing where I am going with this? There was a season in my teaching career where teaching became a way for me to show what I could do, a way to show how good my class was doing. It was a way to indirectly proclaim, "Look at what we're doing." When the focus shifted to this shady goal of trying to make a name for myself in teaching, pressure started seeping through the cracks of my tainted perspective. Before I knew it, I was caught in the comparison trap. If another teacher was doing something, then I felt like I *had* to do it too (you know, gotta keep up). If I had a parent tell me good things about another teacher, I felt like I *had* to show I was 'good enough' too. I innately put this pressure on myself for no apparent reason. This showed me I had lost perspective on what teaching was all about. Teaching is a gift, an act of service for others. Once I took my focus off trying to 'keep up' or be '*the one*' teacher parents wanted, I could enjoy my gift of teaching. Once I accepted the truth, I didn't **need** affirmation from others to validate who I was. The pressure was released, and I became eager to serve selflessly.

When I start feeling 'off' and those unfavorable emotions seem to get a grip on my mind, I try to press into prayer. I ask God to help me not **need** affirmation from others to pursue excellence. Coming from a woman whose love language is words of affirmation, it's hard. It's like I am hardwired to want to hear praise and positive feedback. But what we must understand is, when our value and success is based on others' feedback, we will never truly have confidence because everyone's opinion can change at any given moment. The only affirmation, foundation, and unchanging truth is what God himself speaks over us. Once we let go of *needing* the approval of others, we will find ourselves less offended, more cooperative, and just happier on the inside. And isn't this what we want? To be filled with joy in what we do? Let's make it a point to not let the enemy steal our joy by having us compete with one another. We have enough challenges as educators as it is; let's make it a point to encourage, help, share, and lift up our fellow partners. Even if no one else sees or knows, God sees. Friends, I would rather get a reward from Him anyways. He truly is the best giver of "every good and perfect gift." James 1:17 (NIV) declares, "Every good and perfect gift is from above, coming down from the Father of the heavenly lights, who does not change like shifting shadows." This verse also gives foreground that God doesn't "change like shifting shadows." We don't have to worry about His affirmation or acceptance changing like people's opinions can so easily do.

We have one of the most demanding jobs which can go unrecognized on multiple levels. We strive to please parents. We hope we are meeting the needs of all learners. We spend time planning and planning for the perfect observation in hopes to have a great evaluation in return. We spend time collaborating, discussing interventions, working on enrichment, planning hands-on activities, which many times don't even happen because we are so rushed with daily tasks. And to add to this stress, we can worry so much about doing 'enough' that we miss the mark completely and lose joy in what we do.

Many times, I found myself worrying over things in such a negative way. I started to feel flustered and unproductive. I had plans, but couldn't execute them. I wanted to do so much, but in reality, I accomplished very little. I found myself wanting to do more than I could handle just to keep up with others. When I catch myself stepping into the comparison trap, I have to quickly stop and ask myself, "Why am I placing such a burden on myself?" If it stems from feelings of negative self-worth or comparison, I know it's not from God. If I am inspired to grow and learn from others out of the pure joy of teaching and sharpening my skills, however, that is the motivation and passion I want to drive me. There is nothing wrong with trying to do our best. We are called to give our best with all our hearts. When we allow what we do to stem from love and pure motives, we find freedom. When we are free from those mental barriers, we will be more at ease with an increased awareness of how to help those around us.

Friend, you are chosen. You are *'the one'* God loves dearly and sees as priceless, one of a kind. You don't have to prove your value or worth to anyone when you know you are already complete in Him.

Colossians 2:10 (NIV) affirms us saying, "and in Christ you have been brought to fullness. He is the head over every power and authority." The easy-to-read translation of this verse says, "We are complete having everything we need." We aren't complete or good enough because we are the most requested teacher. We aren't *the one* because parents, colleagues, or administration thinks so. Actually, *we are complete because we belong to Christ.*

Having affirmation and encouragement from others is motivating, heartwarming, and appreciated. Who wouldn't want encouragement from others? We just need to guard our hearts and minds from thinking we **need** those things to affirm our worth. How freeing would it be if our motivation, confidence, and value came from knowing we are *already complete*, having everything we need *because* we belong to Christ. You are enough now. You are #TheOne God has uniquely chosen. You are not overlooked. Let God remind You there is no need to prove yourself to anyone.

POWER POINTS

Colossians 2:10
Colossians 3:23-24
Luke 9:46
James 1:17

POWER MOMENT

Lord, I thank You that when thoughts of insecurity or comparison creep in, I can remember Your promise that I am complete now, having everything I need because I belong to You. Fill me with Your confidence. Keep my heart steadfast and focused on doing my best for You, trusting You will handle the rest. Help me to be a colleague who encourages and builds others up. I pray that I would lay down any offense or disappointment and allow You to take the lead and resolve any situations. Help me to share my knowledge with those around me as I continue to learn from others as well. I pray You would give me the freedom to be myself. Thank You, God, for renewing my mind. In Jesus' name, amen.

SMART GOALS

Select - Choose a verse to meditate on. Write it below.

_____

_____

_____

Marinate - Once you have chosen a verse, let it sink into your spirit. What thoughts or impressions do you feel the Holy Spirit is revealing to you?

_____

_____

_____

Ask- Ask God for clarity and wisdom as you finish up the day's reading. Ask what He would like you to do or improve. Ask Him for help if there is an area of need or a way you can bless someone else in need.

_____

_____

_____

Reveal- What has God revealed to you during this devotional time? Write down any thoughts or revelations.

_____

_____

_____

Take action- What is a practical step you can take after reading today's chapter or selected verse?

_____

_____

_____

#ForSuchaTimeasThis

"Does it make sense to pray for guidance about the future if we are not obeying in the thing that lies before us today? How many momentous events in Scripture depended on one person's seemingly small act of obedience! Rest assured: Do what God tells you to do now, and, depend upon it, you will be shown what to do next."[12]

Elisabeth Elliot

The myriad of reasons teachers are leaving the classroom setting is long. Each reason is warranted and one hundred percent understandable. It doesn't take much scroll time to read an article being shared by a parent, educator, or random person expressing the concern for the downward spiral in today's educational system. It seems like all the odds keep stacking themselves up against us. More than ever, keeping well-intended, high-quality teachers in a profession with so many challenges seems almost impossible to do. Nevertheless, there is hope and a future to think about, even during #SuchaTimeasThis.

I recently read posts from people declaring why they were leaving the teaching profession. As stated previously, each point was valid. But, can I tell you my gut response and my honest-to-God thought? The very reason you want to leave is the very reason I feel called to stay. I don't know what God will have me doing in the future. I do not know where the road leads to later in life, but for now, it's in the classroom…for such a time as this.

I am not trying to be a martyr for the teaching profession. I have not been brainwashed to think I have no other choice. I do not feel as though I have to continue. On the contrary, I see God has given me the *opportunity to continue*. I am an everyday woman. I wash my hair when I can, constantly wonder if I forgot something; I'm a mom to five sons, an Army wife. I am a woman who has questioned her sanity more than once, who constantly questions her choices. I make mistakes, wonder if I do enough, and somehow, despite all of my short-comings, am loved by a gracious God who has placed me in this vocation for His purpose. Before anyone thinks I am trying to give up my family life, time, and sanity because I am trying to make a name for myself, let me assure you, it is not the aim. I understand this is where God has me for now, where He may have you as well. I understand teaching is not for everyone, but my prayer is the years I give to education are purposeful. An effective, purpose-driven heart can only happen with God as the inspiration.

Let's also just get this point out of the way: whether we stay in the educational system or leave, it does not make us any better or worse than someone else. Remember, we all have our own race to run. Anyone who is getting ready to leave teaching has the right and the responsibility to leave knowing what is best for their spiritual, mental, emotional, and physical well-being. There is no shaming, no judgment at all for anyone who leaves teaching. I am reminded of the saying, "If momma ain't happy, no one is happy." Educators are put in strenuous circumstances, financial hardships, and just flat out hard times. If changing careers is what God has led someone to do, I will root for them. There's a lot of pain and damage which can happen if an educator stays in a profession where their heart and mind have checked out. There can be internal mental turmoil and external ripple effects. This is true for *any* profession. The hard part of teaching is that our outlook, attitude, and work ethic affects more than just ourselves. Some of us teach at least twenty different students a day (and that's if we have a small class size, which is not the norm). That's a lot of individuals who can be affected by just one person daily. Even guiding just *one* person is a huge responsibility. Keep in mind, our attitudes will shape our performance, and how we view different situations. Better to hold onto truth than to sink in misery.

So, before we continue, take heart, my friend. If you are still in the trenches of teaching; there is hope. And if you are working your way out, may God bless you with favorable days ahead. No matter what, God says, "There is surely a future hope for you, and your hope will not be cut off" (Proverbs 23:18, NIV). The New Living Translation says, "You will be rewarded for this; your hope will not be disappointed."

Just pause and read those verses again.

There IS a future hope; it will not be cut off; we will not be disappointed. You will be rewarded.

Queen Esther lived in a time when those of Jewish descent were about to face complete annihilation. Somehow, through God's sovereign, meticulous ways, a hidden, everyday Jewish girl named Esther was placed and chosen to be the wife of King Xerxes, a very powerful and rich ruler. What makes this story even more intriguing was how God placed Esther, a Jew, to become the wife of King Xerxes during the *exact* time there would be this mandate to extermi-nate the Jews in the land. Mordecai, Esther's cousin, sent word to her letting her know how King Xerxes had just signed a mandate to "destroy, kill and annihilate all the Jews—young and old, women and children—on a single day, the thirteenth day of the twelfth month, the month of Adar, and to plunder their goods" (Esther 3:13 NIV). Knowing her unique position to the King, Mordecai asked Queen Esther to step up and speak to the King on their behalf. (I am sure many of you know this story, but if not, head over to the book of Esther and read the story yourself. It is a short read, and such a great depiction of God's divine mastery of His grand plan in our lives).

In a nutshell, Esther wasn't very thrilled to speak up to the King. In ancient times, if the king did not summon the queen to his presence, she could be ex-ecuted for coming to him without permission. She let Mordecai (her cousin) know about her fear and reluctance, and his response spoke to her then and speaks to us now. In Esther 4:14b (NIV) Mordecai exclaims, "And who knows but that you have come to your royal position for such a time as this?" One reason this story is relevant to our lives today is what her position represents. She was placed in a situation to have an impact. If Queen Esther refused to see the need and step up, thousands upon thousands would have been killed by her complacency. Her position allowed her to do for a nation what they could not do for themselves. Our position holds significance as well.

God:
1. Placed Esther as the Queen to King Xerxes.
2. Used Esther's position to make a difference.
3. Made Himself real to her and those around her.

God:
1. Placed us where we are in our careers. God can use any situation for His glory and purpose.

2. Uses our position daily to make a difference (however "little" or "big" the difference, we have been given an opportunity).
3. Will make Himself real to us and show Himself to those around us.

We may not be a king or queen of a nation, but we are sons and daughters to a mighty God who is the King of Kings. Therefore, we have royalty in our blood. Every moment, every situation, every experience we have gone through in life can be viewed as moments passing us by, or moments we use purposefully. How unfortunate it would be to view our lives as mere accidents or luck of the draw. We may not be in a 'royal' position (I get it), but we are still in a position of extremely high importance. What we do with our current positions can either propel others or stunt growth.

We have been placed in this position to make a difference (academically, behaviorally, socially, mentally; the impact teachers have is immense) and make Jesus known to those around us. We can do this by encouraging students who feel like they can't learn, supporting our colleagues when they are struggling with life, or simply need a helping hand; participating in the solution, not the problem; showing what it looks like to serve in excellence, just as He would, giving our best even when no one sees. I love the way 2 Corinthians 3:3 (TPT) describes our role as being, "living letters written by Christ, not with ink but by the Spirit of the living God—not carved onto stone tablets but on the tablets of tender hearts." We are Christ's *living letters* to others.

This doesn't mean we always get it right or always feel like coming to work all chipper and giddy (trust me, I get it!). This doesn't mean we are perfect, and we won't have our moments. However, it *does* mean our seemingly 'little' teaching job has great significance and responsibility. Maybe we don't hold a 'royal' position by the world's standards, but I truly believe God sees our work as a high calling to represent Him and bring change. Think about it, *we are influencing the next generations*. This in itself is a huge calling, not to be taken lightly. God has positioned us in this career to make a difference. We must see we have been called to make an impact *for such a time as this*. Even if you are getting ready to leave the profession or unsure you have what it takes, keep in mind that in the meantime, we are still responsible for the now. Do your best now. Live on purpose now. Be intentional now while we wait and expect great things from the Lord. We hope for His hand to help us. We trust in His sovereign plan for our lives.

These teaching moments aren't an accident. What if God brought you here, with this class, with that one student, with your child, because only you had the ability to make the difference? What if the struggle wasn't to change someone else, but to change you, to deepen your faith, and bring you closer to Him through the experience?

Friends, it's scary to see what is happening to our educational system. It breaks my heart to see educators being pressed down on from all sides. It takes courage and heart to even see good, but I promise it's there. God says there is a future hope, it will not be cut off, and we will not be disappointed. Let us come together as educators to give our best in the meantime: to speak up when we must, be wise with our choice of words, and focused on making a change even when it is contrary to the norm. God will give us insight and ideas to make a difference if we press into Him and believe for change and direction. God changes our perspective and outlook on life because we start seeing through His lens and not the world. We may be the only teacher seeing a solution when others can't. We may be the one teacher who is willing to speak up for what's right when others won't. We may be the one teacher who takes time out of our busy schedule and helps, prays for, or supports another person. God may even give you the grace to work with a difficult colleague. We have been placed where we are for such a time as this.

The perfect year will never happen. I mean, there might be the 'good ol' days' we reminisce about, but perfect, that's a stretch. Each day we are placed within a work environment that is either a learning experience for ourselves or an opportunity for us to better someone else. If we can hold onto this perspective when the stormy days come, it will help us in how we react, speak, and think of our future. Just like Queen Esther, we have the choice to make a positive difference where we are or we can choose to let life and its struggles silence our voice and strip us of any good expectations. God has the power to help us make a difference in what we do. We can overcome challenges that arise against us when we stay in step with His guidance.

I also want to insert this plug: God understands we have tender hearts. Consider 2 Corinthians 3:3 that says we are living letters of Christ, and His words are written by the Spirit on our *tender hearts*. There is no way, for any sane human being to find good in all that is going on with teaching at times. However, God takes our tender hearts, knowing how fragile they are, and equips us with the Gospel of the Good News, promises of hope and a future to give us the strength to continue. Psalm 73:26 (NIV) reassures, "My flesh and my heart may fail, but God is the strength of my heart and my portion forever." Trust Him for strength, the courage to make a difference, and the hope for a blessed future. Just as Queen Esther moved past her feelings of reluctance and reaped a great breakthrough in doing so, we move past any negative feelings and remember we have been placed where we are for a purpose. We can't trust our feelings, but we can trust God will not waste anything we do for His purpose and His glory. Guiding and leading the next generation is a high calling; let us do so in excellence.

POWER POINTS

Proverbs 23:18
Psalm 73:26
2 Corinthians 3:3
Esther 3:13

POWER MOMENT

God, thank You for time, time to live and be the change the world needs. Thank You for the time and ability to make a difference. Thank you for the opportunity to work and have a position for such a time as this. Holy Spirit, put perspective back into my heart. Give me the desire and passion to work in such a way that others can see Your hand moving on my behalf. When circumstances would dictate otherwise, Lord, may You give me hope to look forward to the future. Right now, I place my profession, workplace, those under my care, and all concerns in Your hand. May I be equipped to serve and work with integrity, bringing You glory and leading others to hope as well. Not on my own strength, but through Your strength, may I climb mountains, expect great things, and see a breakthrough in any challenge. Move on my behalf. Fill my cup with purpose so I don't lose sight of my 'why.' Mighty Warrior, give me the tools, wisdom, insight, and power to move forward and make a difference. In Jesus' name, amen!

SMART GOALS

Select - Choose a verse to meditate on. Write it below.

_____

_____

_____

Marinate - Once you have chosen a verse, let it sink into your spirit. What thoughts or impressions do you feel the Holy Spirit is revealing to you?

_____

_____

_____

Ask- Ask God for clarity and wisdom as you finish up the day's reading. Ask what He would like you to do or improve. Ask Him for help if there is an area of need or a way you can bless someone else in need.

_____

_____

_____

Reveal- What has God revealed to you during this devotional time? Write down any thoughts or revelations.

_____

_____

_____

Take action- What is a practical step you can take after reading today's chapter or selected verse?

_____

_____

_____

#EnjoytheNow

"It is not how much we have, but how much we enjoy, that makes happiness."[13]

Charles Spurgeon

I've spent some time in a cloudy haze of dissatisfaction. I got so caught up in stories about other people's successes making tons of money, working from home, traveling the world, or seemingly having it all together. It just made my teacher life seem so insufficient, less than enough, not fulfilling, simply not what I wanted to be doing anymore. The more I stared at their lives, the more I steered in a direction not aligned with where God placed me.

I will preface this chapter by stating: there is nothing wrong with chasing dreams, having goals, and reaching for new opportunities. All of these things are great; actually, most teachers I know have some sort of side gig. Truth is, many times we aren't getting paid what is due us. I welcome residual income (Extra cash? Yes! Give me some!). This topic is not undermining us having side jobs, businesses, etc. Today, I come to you with a cup of self-reflection and a thought-provoking question. Does social media, marketing, images, or knowledge of other people's accomplishments spark thoughts of comparison? How about dissatisfaction with your current status or uneasiness in your current role or position in life? Are we pursuing other roles and not being faithful to what God has given us now? It's uncomfortable for me to admit, but there have been times when I have envied what others were doing in their lives. I wanted the ability to wear 'fuzzy slippers' (ok not literally, but you know what I mean) and stay home, have a laptop on my lap (specifically a MacBook Pro, cause c'mon, everyone who's anyone has one, right?), sip on my coffee, and exhale saying, "Living the dream."

However, for now, this is not my current status. And somehow, my real life as a teacher started to look more and more dreary than delightful. Somehow,

I found myself trying to find ways out, and giving less intentionality to where I was at the moment. Listen, I am all about earning more and following our passions and dreams, but as educators, we have a tremendous responsibility to not neglect what we have been entrusted with **now**. Even if it means we have to get up, dress up, and show up every morning ready to mold minds, this is our position now. Our hearts' cry should be for God to give us joy in our current role and position, even if we are pursuing another goal. This ideology may not be popular since we are surrounded by images propagandizing chasing our dreams, following our hearts (which again, I don't believe is wrong), but our dreams and goals need to be aligned with God's will and His timing. Too many times, we are looking ahead to what's next, and we shortchange our current moments and give less of ourselves. My less-than-best attitude and effort can result in students getting half of what I can offer and half of what they need. Our time now is not wasted, friends. Our role is not only crucial in our own lives, but also in the lives of those we encounter every single day. I read this verse during a devotional one morning, and I straight up had to stop and reread it like ten times. Let's see if you get stuck on a certain part too:

*If God gives some people wealth, property, and the power to enjoy those things, they should enjoy them. They should accept the things they have and **enjoy their work—that is a gift from God**. People don't have many years to live, so they must remember these things all their life. God will keep them busy with **the work they love to do**.*
Ecclesiastes 5:19-20 (ERV, emphasis added)

The Message translation reads:

Yes, we should make the most of what God gives, both the bounty and the capacity to enjoy it, accepting what's given and delighting in the work. It's God's gift! God deals out joy in the present, the now.

Reflect on those last words, "God deals out joy in the present, the *now*."

So, I may have given you a hint to the part that stuck out to me, but do you see how God actually *wants* us to enjoy our work? It's called a gift from God. When I read those verses, I couldn't help but confess to God how many times I haven't enjoyed my job, how many times I've compared my life to others or wanted something totally different. I admitted I was drained, tired, and running on empty. I confessed that I was going through the motions with no enjoyment.

AT. ALL.

Friends, we've probably all been there. Maybe some of us are there right now, yearning for something else.

What are the reasons you have mentally and emotionally checked out? There may be several reasons an educator is done; comparison, feeling unfulfilled, financial stresses, behavior issues, lack of support, or simply being tired of circumstances getting worse. Whatever the reason, no matter how big or small, I encourage you today to ask God to renew your vision and perspective. Whatever the reason, I believe God is still able to bring joy instead of mourning, to exchange beauty for ashes, and to refresh us with renewed strength.

Isaiah 44:3 (NLT) holds such a sweet promise. It reads, "For I will pour out water to quench your thirst and to irrigate your parched fields." Our career as teachers can sometimes feel like a parched field. It can feel dry, draining, and even empty; yet, through God's word, He gives us promises to give us a drink to keep us going. He will quench our thirst. He will provide "streams for dry ground." This verse can be useful in all aspects of our lives, but today, I want to focus on our profession. I want us to think about the turns education has taken and how it has made many of us feel like quitting, completely dry on the inside.

Friends, when I found myself lost and apathetic towards my role as a teacher, I had to have a serious heart-to-heart with the Lord. I had to beg Him for passion again. I just didn't feel it anymore, and it was affecting my planning, work ethic, and attitude. My heart just wasn't into it, and when my intentions were not there, it affected my daily routines. I knew better, but I got used to the routine of teaching and I accepted it as my new norm. I did the same ol' things because they didn't require much thought or effort. I knew the standards so well that I didn't go above and beyond because why should I? Check in and check out. Just do what I need to do in order to get by. How sad. How sad I let the system get to me, but it happens. Yet, something deep inside of me was unsettled. I knew this style of mediocre teaching and attitude didn't fit me. It wasn't the person I wanted to be. I had to ask God to help me see past what others were doing, my current feelings, and whatever other goals I had in mind, and I had to remember I was called to give my best *now* not just *when*.

I wish I could tell you after I prayed, I felt passionate again with teaching, but it would be a lie. This prayer wasn't something I said once and moved on; it became a daily prayer that He answered over time (and *still* answers when my feelings wane). It took time for me to 'feel' it, but I am sure He answered me right away, it just took time for my feelings to catch up.

Our life wasn't meant to be lived in dread or despair. Sometimes, part of the problem is our outlook. It can seem so dreary, we don't see hope, or we forget to pray about things like our heart towards teaching. As the fictional C.S. Lewis said in the movie *Shadowlands*, "I pray because I can't help myself. I pray because I'm helpless. I pray because the need flows out of me all the time, waking and sleeping. It doesn't change God. *It changes me.*"[14] Prayer changes us. It changes our perspective. It changes our hearts. It changes our views. It changes us. We may not always be able to control class sizes, the kids placed in our classroom, who we work with, or what curriculum is being used, but we can change ourselves with the power of the Holy Spirit and His spiritual truths!

If you are still currently working in the education field and haven't left, I encourage you to hold onto spiritual truths to keep you grounded during the temperamental changes of emotions while teaching. You, my friend, are too valuable and important to waste any moment of life to chance or circumstance. You have the power to decide now how your outlook and mindset will be. The mindset of unhappiness and discontentment can blind us from seeing any good around us; however, **through Christ**, we have the ability to slow down and take our thoughts captive. 2 Corinthians 10:5 (ESV, emphasis added) states, "We destroy arguments and every lofty opinion raised against the knowledge of God and **take every thought captive** to obey Christ." Maybe some thoughts we need to take captive are lies such as:

My job isn't as important as someone else's.
If I had more than I would be happy.
Being a teacher has no value.
This job will never get better.
I will always struggle and have the worst situations.
I will be happy when…(How many times do we look to the future for happiness instead of finding good in the now?)

The verse 2 Corinthians 10:5 is crucial because it gives us a springboard to bounce off the negative emotions and thoughts which try to keep us in a pit of despair. I am not saying things aren't hard or challenging. I am not saying we do not have reason to feel what we feel. But if we only focus on justifying ourselves, we may find ourselves stuck in negativity which in turn will affect our performance and attitude. I will speak for myself and say, staying stuck in a pit never got me anywhere but deeper in a hole. When we take our thoughts captive to obey Christ, it means we remember that the word of God says He is for us not against us (Romans 8:31). He said He would be our defender and fight our battles (Exodus 14:14). Therefore, when I choose to focus on anything, I choose (with the help of the Spirit) to focus on His words, not my fluctuating feelings. He will give us insight on what not to do, what to do, and when *to do* it. Honestly, His ways always work out better.

With each school year comes new students, new circumstances, new parents, and new challenges. Some years, we feel like we finally get the hang of things, while other years, we walk through the valley of the shadow of death...yeah, it can be bad, I know.

However, verses like Ecclesiastes 5:19-20 confirm that God wants us to enjoy what we have; enjoying the work we do is a gift from Him. If He wants us to be joyful, then let's ask Him to help us regain joy for the things we are doing *now* so we can truly appreciate and revel in future blessings. The same God who appoints the sun to shine by day and the moon and stars to shine by night also has the power to control our emotional well-being (Jeremiah 31:35 NLT). His word confirms there can be joy in our work. Joy in the now.

I can't help but ask God how this fits into our everyday jobs. I know many of you reading this book want to enjoy what you do, and I believe God can and will help us find joy in the now, not just:

When I have the "high performing" class, I will be better.
When I don't have students with behavioral issues, I can enjoy the year.
When the admin supports the staff more, I can enjoy the workplace better.
When parents start supporting their kids and teachers, I can enjoy what I do.

Maybe we have legitimate reasons not to love our jobs. Maybe after having that 'one class' and being left exhausted each day, we vowed teaching was not for us. Or, maybe it's been an accumulation of years consisting of headaches and trying to do too much, leaving us empty and dry on the inside. Wherever we find ourselves on the spectrum, I am here to say, God can and will bring enjoyment back into what we do when we give Him the chance to work. We may not instantly 'feel' joyful, and circumstances may seem unchanged, but many times the biggest change will start in our heart and mindset. Placing our hope not in the 'when' but in 'Who' makes a huge difference in our mental and emotional health. This mind shift has saved me from hopelessness too many times to count.

We can pray for joy now and ask God to handle what we can't. Trust me, He sees the issues. He knows our struggle, and in His might, while He's taking up our case, He can give us His gift of enjoying what we do. The first step is taking God at His word and meditating on the scriptures. Let the verses sink into your heart, knowing it is possible to have joy amidst the struggle. If we are lacking joy, fulfillment in our career, let's go to The One who has what we need. I choose to believe if God promises joy in our work, then somehow, it is possible. Somehow, it is possible for us to find joy in our profession even amidst trial, exhaustion, and frustration. The same God who made rivers in the desert can bring life and fulfillment in our careers.

Personally speaking, this is where conviction comes in. I had to be truly honest with myself on where I was in life. I had to address any issues of comparison and dissatisfaction and root out any possible causes which may have been drowning my purpose. Was I justified in feeling drained? Yes. I can't begin to account for all of the things I see and hear about what educators go through. Unfair is an understatement. However, what I have learned and am still learning is that God works from the inside out. Meaning, even through chaos and uncertainty, I can place my hope and expectation in His character. Why would He tell me to have joy in Him if He is not able to fulfill His promise? The more I find myself focused on the unjust and unfair situations, the less capable I am of seeing change or even expecting change. I actually find myself shutting down and becoming more complacent. Maybe it's just a me thing, but focusing on what I cannot control makes me feel emotionally out of control.

Seeking God's counsel and joy gives us the wisdom to rise up and speak up when change is needed. Doing things out of anger and bitterness may give us the motivation to act, but not in the most appropriate or effective ways.

If you are planning to leave or stay in teaching, one thing remains the same: God wants you to enjoy what you do. Seem impossible? I think humanly speaking, it is. It is when things don't make sense. But when we come to terms that it is by His grace, His strength that we enjoy whatever comes, we can expect the impossible to become possible. I love what Jesus says in Luke 18:27 (NIV),

"What is impossible with man is possible with God." Let us not put limits on our limitless God.

What are we going to do now knowing the truth of His word? What will we do with what God has said in His word? How do we want this school year, the next school year to be? Will we take God at His word and expect Him to fill our cups with joy, even though…(you fill in the blank). Will we believe He is able to do the impossible? Maybe we just need to take the time to take it to Him personally. Maybe we need to slow down and have a heart-to-heart with our Creator so He can bring back the joy which has been lost in the shuffle of life. No matter what we are feeling, we can give it to Him. Trust me, He won't be surprised or caught off guard. He knows our frustrations, sees our hearts' desires and wants to give us joy in what we are doing. Whether it is teaching, being a caregiver, mentoring others, or anything else, it is a gift from God. Let us not let the world steal our joy. What God gives us, no one can take away.

Let me leave you with one more beautiful reminder from the word of God. 2 Chronicles 32:8 (NLT) shows King Hezekiah encouraging his people over a battle they were facing against the king of Assyria who had a vast army. King Hezekiah tells his discouraged people, "'He may have a great army, but they are merely men. We have the LORD our God to help us and to fight our battles for us!' Hezekiah's words greatly encouraged the people." Friends, the odds may be stacked against us. We may feel like the opposition and demands are too much, but we have the Lord our God to help us fight our battles. Keep fighting the good fight of faith and excellence, dear friend. God will not disappoint us. He is greater. Yes, He will provide the motivation to continue and to #Enjoy-theNow.

POWER POINTS

Ecclesiastes 5:19-20
Jeremiah 31:35
Luke 18:27
2 Corinthians 10:5
Isaiah 44:3a
2 Chronicles 32:8

POWER MOMENT

God, you know the struggle. You see each teacher and the story each one of us carries. There may be burdens I carry which no one else knows about or understands, but I believe what seems like an impossible request can be made possible through Your power. Father, may I experience fulfillment and excitement in what I do. It is a gift from You for me to enjoy the work I do. Lord, I want this gift and ask for joy, not joy based on circumstances alone, but a joy which comes from deep within, joy from You. Help me be happy. Yes, happy. God cheer any discouraged or disheartened heart. Do what only You can do: restore joy in my life and help me work in excellence, not complacency. Lord, please take this battle, any situation, and turn it around for good. I pray for supernatural joy, peace, encouragement, and favor by the power of the Holy Spirit. In Jesus' name, amen!

SMART GOALS

Select - Choose a verse to meditate on. Write it below.

_____

_____

_____

Marinate - Once you have chosen a verse, let it sink into your spirit. What thoughts or impressions do you feel the Holy Spirit is revealing to you?

_____

_____

_____

Ask- Ask God for clarity and wisdom as you finish up the day's reading. Ask what He would like you to do or improve. Ask Him for help if there is an area of need or a way you can bless someone else in need.

_____

_____

_____

Reveal- What has God revealed to you during this devotional time? Write down any thoughts or revelations.

_____

_____

_____

Take action- What is a practical step you can take after reading today's chapter or selected verse?

_____

_____

_____

#DailyBread

"You may have to fight a battle more than once to win it."[15]

Margaret Thatcher

Daily.

Give us this day our *daily* bread.

When looking into the Lord's prayer recorded both in Matthew 6:9-13 and Luke 11:2-4, we see Jesus, after acknowledging who God is and giving Him honor, requesting *daily bread*. The first thing Jesus asks for is daily bread. This appeal makes me stop and think about its importance. Why this specific petition first? He could have asked for anything, yet this was His first request. The term 'bread' symbolizes both physical and spiritual attributes of provision. In the Old Testament, we see first-hand God sending down "bread from heaven" (manna) to help meet the physical needs of His people (Exodus 16:4). However, we also know from scripture we do not live by bread alone, *but by every word of God* (Matthew 4:4 NLT). More specifically, John 6:33 (NLT) tells us, "The true bread of God is the one who comes down from heaven and gives life to the world."

We may have physical needs (for which God will provide), but we cannot live just off physical provision. Our spiritual, mental, and emotional health matters to God as well. How do we feed our spiritual hunger and thirst? By every word of God. Jesus is asking the Father to give Him the daily bread needed to sustain physical and spiritual life. We see the correlation between the physical and spiritual side of God's provision in Isaiah 55:10-11 (NLT):

The rain and snow come down from the heavens and stay on the ground to water the earth. They cause the grain to grow, producing seed for the farmer and bread for the hungry. It is the same with my word. I send it out, and it always produces fruit. It will accomplish all I want it to, and it will prosper everywhere I send it.

God's mighty word is truth; it is living, powerful, and able to bring life to dead situations. The word of God is alive, active, and filled with promises for us to take hold of. His promises equip us with spiritual nutrients, wisdom, and divine armor. It is where we attain revelation of Who He is, and what we are called to do. As Psalm 119:105 (NLT) clearly points out, "Your word is a lamp to guide my feet and a light for my path." One very crucial element in our walk with God is spending time in His word. It allows us to know His heart and character, learn what He asks of us, and understand His ways. When we do not place His word (our daily bread) as a priority, we tend to starve our spirit which leaves us vulnerable for mental and emotional breakdowns.

I know for a fact, when I am physically famished, anything and everything looks good and I can go on an all-out junk food binge. The problem with this is it is temporary satisfaction with negative side effects. Headaches, stomach pains, bloating…you get the point, right?

The same is true with our spiritual self. When we are spiritually dry and running on empty, certain things can seem good to stew on: bitterness, anger, rage, self-pity, despair, discouragement. Certain things such as a clash with a colleague, someone being unappreciative, a student with behavioral issues, or not having enough time (just to name a few), can all be a breaking point leading us into a downward spiral of hopelessness. When we feed our spirit, we strengthen our faith muscles to better walk in belief. We start to nourish our hopes and realization of who God is, which drives us to accomplish challenging tasks through His grace and strength. If we are not grounded and fed by His daily bread, we will be more inclined to focus on the negative, which in return, can poorly influence our behavior.

Asking our heavenly Father to give us daily bread signifies some important principles. First, we acknowledge Him as our Provider for all things. Secondly, we recognize that His word renews our minds. Ephesians 4:23 (NLT) reminds us to "let the Spirit renew your thoughts and attitudes." The Spirit of God lives inside us, but we must take time to study His word for mental regeneration to take place. The battle to have a healthy mindset is an ongoing task. I don't think anyone *always* has a positive mindset and outlook. I think we can improve our perspective and gain clarity, but this is not something that stays consistent without intentionality. In the Amplified Bible, Ephesians 4:23 tells us to "be *continually* renewed in the spirit of your mind [having a fresh, untarnished mental and spiritual attitude]."

We face multiple facets of emotions which attach themselves to our career. We do not just teach core curriculum; we teach life and social skills, growth mindset, responsibility, positive character traits, and anger management 101. These unwritten set of standards can take a toll on our already filled brains and long lesson plans. Many times, we can feel as though our voice, our stance, and our mission is all done in vain, falling on deaf ears, with no fruit in sight. There are many examples in the Bible of people just like us who were called by the Lord to do a great work (teaching is a great work), yet their labor was not welcomed or appreciated. The prophet Isaiah gives us some food for thought, some insight into the depth of emotions many have faced in the past and still face today.

Let me paint a backdrop for what was going on here. The prophet Isaiah was given the assignment to prophesy the coming of the Messiah, Jesus Christ, and speak truth to the nation of Israel. As we will soon see, even prophets from the Lord question their calling and purpose. In Isaiah 49:4 (NLT) Isaiah converses with the Lord and exclaims, "'But my work seems so useless! I have spent my strength for nothing and to no purpose. Yet I leave it all in the Lord's hand; I will trust God for my reward.'"

It seems odd for this account of the prophet Isaiah to strike a chord with me, but it hits home. I find consolation knowing someone else has felt the emotional struggle of questioning their role and career. It was Isaiah's job to tell of the Messiah's coming even if no one listened, even if it wasn't a highly-respected profession, and even if he didn't receive public praise. He voiced a concern I too have felt. If you've been in the educational arena for even one day, you may have experienced the backlash or lack of support from parents. Maybe it was an administrator or possibly a fellow colleague who somehow left you feeling pretty beat up emotionally. Sometimes, it can be the unappreciative mannerisms of our own students that make us feel drained and insignificant.

I am sure we as teachers can relate to the overwhelming, tired ache the prophet Isaiah must have felt pursuing his calling. I am sure he questioned if he had really heard from God. I am sure he wondered why he was even doing what he was doing or if he was on the right track. Whatever the source, whatever the reason, there is a glimmer of hope:

1. You are not alone.
2. God understands.
3. He will be our great reward.

Isaiah started off his complaint with turbulence and discouragement, yet he resolved to remind himself what he needed to do: leave it in the Lord's hand and trust God for his reward. Both things are beautifully said and necessary for emotional and mental stability. How do we leave it in the Lord's hand? We decide to commit to praying, filling our cup with daily doses of His Word, and mentally reminding ourselves of His promises. Even if we feel like we can't let go, we tell Him (and ourselves) He is in charge. We spend time in His word renewing our minds. I do not have a secret magic formula to give things to God, but I do strive to take God at His word. Some days are harder than others, but we fight the good fight of faith, even if it is a daily choice to believe His promises. Inspired by the words of Charles Spurgeon, Christian singer-songwriter Babbie Mason penned the beautiful song "Trust His Heart."[16] The chorus says, "God is too good to be unkind and He is too wise to be mistaken. And when we cannot trace His hand, we must trust His heart." We get to know God's heart by spending time in His word. Right now, reading this devotional, taking time to learn His word and meditate on key scripture, is a step toward leaving things in the Lord's hands, trusting that He can be trusted, trusting in His sovereign plan for your life, and believing what you are doing is not done in vain. Leaving things in His hands and knowing He is working things out on our behalf can be a big step toward mental calmness. It frees us from feeling like we are going nowhere fast. No day, intervention, or #teachertired day is wasted when given to Him.

Constant prayer and constant surrender (not easy to our flesh) are where I have found my biggest breakthrough and deliverance. Remember, even if we feel like we can't just "let go and let God," His grace is sufficient to help us when we can't do things for ourselves. "'My grace is all you need. My power works best in weakness,'" is the response given by God to the apostle Paul in 2 Corinthians 12:9 (NLT), after he repeatedly went to God for help. If God said it, He can back up His words. *Lord, I pray you show us grace and power when we struggle to leave things in Your hands.*

I do not know the specific battle you are facing. I do not know what hardships you are going through this year, but I believe when we fight the good fight of faith, believing there is purpose in what we do, nothing is done in vain. Keep drawing near to God for guidance; He will give you mental and emotional clarity to finish strong…maybe tired too, but stronger in character. You will be wiser for the future and able to lend a helping hand to another friend who may need a battle buddy.

Isaiah 49:4 also includes a reminder to "trust God for my reward." When we are up against what seems like a negative eclipse, shadowing any goodness in the teaching profession, this right here helps: it helps to trust God for our reward. It helps to know God is our compensator. What others may overlook and take for granted, He will not. When we can remind ourselves of Who controls the outcome of our lives, it gives our minds mental ease. Focusing on Jesus, our Lord and Savior, feeds our spirit. Our mental health is worth fighting for one day at a time.

Here's the reality: having a Godly calling and purpose doesn't mean it will always be easy. I have learned many times, a calling from God doesn't exempt us from challenges and pain. There will be hard moments, but there is *still* good in the hard. When challenges, pain, or hurt arise, it does not mean God is away from us. The "good" Isaiah is focusing on is God's sovereignty, His ultimate power to help and defend Isaiah's cause. Isaiah is leaning on the hope that God sees him and will redeem him. When we are offended by others, do we revert back to The One who is our Defender, or do we hone in and focus on the offense? Do we believe God will ultimately have the last word on our behalf, or are we defined by what someone did or said about us? Isaiah did not waste the next verse to give credit to his adversary; no, he placed his pain, hope, and expectation on God, who is Ruler over every power and authority. Let us remember to find our strength and daily bread in God each and every day.

POWER POINTS

Matthew 4:4
John 6:33
Isaiah 49:4
Isaiah 55:10-11

Psalm 119:105
Ephesians 4:23
2 Corinthians 12:9

POWER MOMENT

Father, thank you for each new day. Thank you that each day has new beginnings, new mercy, and never-ending grace to fuel my soul. Lord, I ask in the name of Jesus that You keep me from taking time for granted. Help me to spend moments recharging my spirit with the power of Your word, our daily bread. I give You this day and the days to come and ask for the wisdom and insight that only You can give. Give me the desire for a deeper relationship with You and teach me what it means to delight myself in You. Thank You for nourishing every part of my life and knowing exactly what I need to flourish. In Jesus' name, amen.

SMART GOALS

Select - Choose a verse to meditate on. Write it below.

_____

_____

_____

Marinate - Once you have chosen a verse, let it sink into your spirit. What thoughts or impressions do you feel the Holy Spirit is revealing to you?

_____

_____

_____

Ask- Ask God for clarity and wisdom as you finish up the day's reading. Ask what He would like you to do or improve. Ask Him for help if there is an area of need or a way you can bless someone else in need.

_____

_____

_____

Reveal- What has God revealed to you during this devotional time? Write down any thoughts or revelations.

_____

_____

_____

Take action- What is a practical step you can take after reading today's chapter or selected verse?

_____

_____

_____

#MutuallyEncouraged

"I alone cannot change the world, but I can cast a stone across the waters to create many ripples."

Unknown

I have met many individuals who have been a breath of fresh air to me. They would help me breathe in encouragement and exhale frustration. The rejuvenating power one person has on another person's life can be extraordinary. As a Trinity, God knew well the dynamic effect of being united and in one accord when He created the gift of relationships. I can't express enough how grateful I am for the colleagues God has allowed me to work with. The certain coworkers I've had as neighboring partners, my down-the-hall confidants, the secretary in the office, each relationship has served a purpose. The relationships I am reflecting on right now are the ones that were my breath of fresh air when I was suffocating from the pressures around me.

When I first started teaching, I will admit I was a hot mess (Aren't we all at some moments?), scrambling to figure out how to put textbook smarts into practice. I was trained to construct ten-point lesson plans. I read and wrote about action research. I studied differentiated learning, Piaget's Cognitive Development stage theory, Erikson's Psychosocial Theory, Kohlberg's Moral Understanding stage theory; you name it, I am sure I went over it. However, no theory prepared me for the demands of being responsible for the development of young minds. Not only was I in charge of how students performed and progressed, but I had to learn how to be great at classroom management if I intended for any learning to occur. Maybe your management isn't inside a classroom, but a home, daycare facility, some shared space. There is no amount of instructional textbooks or lessons that compare to the value of hands-on learning. Hence, when I first started teaching, I was in dire need of help. I didn't have a clue how to implement centers or engaging activities while keeping my class under control with good time management skills. There was just so much more to this teaching thing than just paperwork. Cue: Mrs. Cisneros and Mrs. Holston, my neighboring teachers.

They were veteran educators who had tons of experience and insight, but most of all, they had passion, like hardcore-on-fire-for-what-you-do kind of passion. Here I was struggling to figure things out, and here they were implementing great lessons and enjoying what they were doing. Don't get me wrong, they had their #teachertired moments too, but something was different. They were passionate and willing to lend a helping hand to someone who obviously was not fully prepared for the challenges of teacher life. There was no sense of competition to outdo one another; there was a genuine concern to share their best practices so that I too could learn and improve. I remember quite well one of my neighboring teachers staying late after school to show me how to organize my classroom library because I had no idea how to even do that. Another colleague suggested I observe her conduct centers because I couldn't seem to grasp the approach. I am a visual learner and needed to see how another person modeled best practices within the classroom.

I learned a great deal of expertise from these outstanding teachers, but most of all, I learned what it looked like to lead with excellence. I learned the value of teamwork and cooperative learning environments, all behind closed doors. They extended a helping hand and encouraged me in ways a textbook never could. They took their own time and made time for me, a new struggling educator. They represented the heart of teaching for me. Even though they were seasoned teachers, they continued to learn best practices, had hearts for service, and were willing to support a fellow colleague without it being in their job description. There was no extra duty pay for the time they spent helping me. They defined a standard of what teamwork represents, and their positive guidance has influenced my decisions ever since.

I worked with these influencers over ten years ago, and here I am writing about it. Why? Because of the effects of their encouragement, example, and passion still ripple in my mind. I'm a better educator because of them, and for that, I am thankful. Our example and service can have a tremendous impact on those around us. 2 Corinthians 5:20a (NLT) tells us, "we are Christ's ambassadors; God is making his appeal through us." How we live our lives represents Him and can either bring life to those around us or hinder others from being their best or seeing God through us. My coworkers, who became my friends early in my teaching career, urged me to be better than I thought I could be and gave me the vision to work in excellence. I found myself wanting to learn more, be better, and grow in my skills to give my best. When we grasp how important our role is to those around us, we will see that our attitude, behaviors, and choices really do affect more than ourselves.

We have been given the opportunity to mutually encourage those we work with. Hebrews 10:24 (NLT) says, "Let us think of ways to motivate one another to acts of love and good works." The New International Version uses the phrase, "spur one another on." The word 'spur' means to propel, encourage, stimulate, or drive something forward. It is a verb. It is an action that we all have been instructed to do in relation to those around us. I am not sure if those teachers ever knew the full extent of their role in developing my work ethic, but their influence helped pave the way for me to serve with purpose.

I share this story with you all to stir your hearts to see ways you too can spur one another on. We know that #teachertired is real and present. Still, we have the power to influence the mindset and attitude of those we work with and those we have in our care. You may not see it, but your drive and push for excellence can incite others to do the same. Your desire to learn more and grow as an educator can spark a flame in those around you. More than ever, our fellow colleagues need that spurring, that modeling, that encouragement to be the best at what we do for His glory and purposes. Our relationships with one another are a big part of our consistent work habits, effort, and impact. We see mutual encouragement needed even with the apostle Paul. In the book of Romans, Paul starts off in chapter one lifting up the Romans and expressing how much their faith and good works have blessed him. Paul writes, "When we get together, I want to encourage you in your faith, but I also want to be encouraged by yours" (Romans 1:12, NLT). The Amplified version of this text reads, "...that we may be mutually encouraged *and* comforted by each other's faith, both yours and mine."

Your passion, your faith, your drive to pursue excellence can be the catalyst that inspires another teacher to do the same. Think of it this way. Have you ever been around a person who was so excited about a product or fitness lifestyle and you saw the changes it was making in their life? Ever feel that urge to ask what they were doing or even find yourself getting inspired to possibly make better health choices as well? Have you ever been in proximity to a go-getter, someone who always went all in at whatever they did? Did it make you reflect and want to push forward to do the same? I have had fellow teacher friends who would post about their love of what they do, and that simple positive reflection would encourage me to see the good in what I was doing as well.

Whether someone is enthusiastic or not, our attitudes do affect those around us. God has called us to live in excellence at whatever we do. Part of that excellence should also be seen in our behavior, outlook, and temperament. Colossians 3:23 (NIV) affirms this by saying, "Whatever you do, work at it with all your heart, as working for the Lord, not for human masters." God didn't say to work at certain things with all our heart or only the things we deem important; no, He said *whatever you do*. Whatever we do could be sitting in a staff meeting for the umpteenth time, where we choose not to gripe and complain, but to be respectful to the presenters. (Again, I've been there before too, but we are trying to set examples of excellence, right?) It could be collaborating with others at our workplace, serving that one person that rubs us the wrong way, or even working to keep our things organized. Whatever we do, we do it as unto the Lord. For many of us, teaching is part of that *whatever we do*. When we do it as unto the Lord, it causes us to check our attitude and raises the bar as to how we perform. How we react and operate represents the One who has called us His own. It challenges us to rise up to His standard, not the worlds.

I will also present the opposite scenario. If we are full of complaining and murmuring, we could perpetuate those negative feelings to rise out of others as well. For example, if we are individuals who constantly voice the negative outlooks over situations at work, we can start a domino effect where many people see murmuring as the sole solution to a problem. If all we see is bleakness around us, that same vision of despondency will extend to those who are in our proximity.

I am reminded of the story of the twelve spies in Numbers 13 who were sent out amongst the Israelites to see the promised land God had vowed to give them. In this chapter, the twelve spies have come back from their mission, and only two of them, Caleb and Joshua, give a favorable report. The other men saw that there was some good in the land, but focused on the challenges and issues, viewing the current inhabitants as too mighty for them to overcome. This negativity spread dread and discouragement into the hearts of their fellow Israelites. Believing in a future and a hope God had promised them seemed more and more unreal. The best part of the story (to me) is when Caleb speaks up. "Then Caleb silenced the people before Moses and said, 'We should go up and take possession of the land, for we can certainly do it'" (Numbers 13:30,

NIV). All it takes is one person to speak up: not argue, not put people and ideas down, but to speak up with confidence and see good even in hard times. Did the people listen to Caleb? Sadly, no. The voices of the naysayers and doubters weighed heaviest in the mind of others who also lacked vision. However, when it came time to enter the promised land, God did not allow those who doubted and complained to enter in. Caleb and Joshua may not have had the support of others, but they got an even greater reward: the promised land. They received the approval from the Lord, and that, my friends, is always going to be greater than any approval from man.

I share this story to give perspective to how powerful our thoughts, words, and actions can be in the lives of those around us. In our everyday working life, how is this 'mutually encouraged' action seen? Well, it can manifest in minor moments, like in our attitudes during staff meetings. For instance, I always seem to feel sorry for presenters who come to speak to us during staff development meetings. I mean, c'mon. We have to admit after a long day of work, the last thing we want to do is listen to someone speak to us. I realize that many times, sitting in meetings, we wish we could be somewhere else, making better use of our time. However, I also understand I cannot expect my own students to be polite and show manners when I teach if I can't extend that same grace to others. I've learned that respect needs to be given at all times, even during staff meetings, whether I want to be there or not, and that my attitude better be one that represents Him well. I haven't always been the best audience nor has my attitude been admirable, but every time my attitude needs an adjustment, the Holy Spirit seems pretty keen to remind me that my attitude, even in this small moment, can encourage others to be respectful, or to complain alongside me.

My prayer and hope is that through seemingly small gestures, we can encourage others to lead and serve in excellence, even in a staff meeting. When there is a problem at work, do we focus on murmuring and talking about the problem (or people), or do we find solutions, working together to lift up ideas and resolutions? How is our everyday attitude encouraging others to better themselves? Paul puts it into perspective for us when he says, "Do not let any unwholesome talk come out of your mouths, but only what is helpful for building others up according to their needs, that it may benefit those who listen" (Ephesians 4:29, NIV). Even our words are called to a higher standard, *that they may benefit those who listen.* We must be mindful that our behavior either encourages others to step up their standard of conduct or causes others to grumble alongside us. I opt to be more like Caleb and Joshua and see victory in situations rather than defeat.

I am not saying to go with the flow and never speak up in opposition. In those situations, we must ask God for His wisdom in our tactfulness and respectfulness when we speak. If we are speaking just to grumble, we never know who else we are discouraging along the way. Let us commit in action and in word, to aim to benefit those around us. We won't always be perfect and get it right. We will have our own moments and frustrations, but now, we will be a little wiser, a little quicker to course-correct if needed. May we take our current position, role, and every opportunity to try our best because we are His ambassadors. Our daily living speaks more about who God is than any amount of words ever could. Do not let the system and mundane tasks of everyday life suck the impact out of who you were called to be. There are people around you who need someone to lead with excellence and that someone is you. Let us be reminded today: we can encourage someone else just by our attitude and passion. The zeal and fervor those teachers exemplified early in my teaching career literally set the bar for how I wanted to be. Be the difference. Someone right now needs your fire to spark their flame again. If you are the one who needs encouragement, remember we can ask God to bring back that passion. Our job is to work with all our heart at *whatever we do*. Our actions will ripple out to others along the way.

POWER POINTS

2 Corinthians 5:20a
Hebrews 10:24
Romans 1:12
Colossians 3:23
Numbers 13:30
Ephesians 4:29

POWER MOMENT

Lord, thank you for the opportunity to teach and inspire others. Many times, I can lose sight of how much influence my words and actions can have on those around me. Help me to lead and serve with excellence. If there is an area in my heart or behavior that needs refining, show me how to improve and bring glory to You in whatever I do. Help me be a blessing to those around me. May my faith encourage others. May You also bring coworkers, friends, and people into my life to encourage me in my effort as a teacher. Thank you for opening my heart to Your word; please help me to be a doer of the word. In Jesus' name, amen.

SMART GOALS

Select - Choose a verse to meditate on. Write it below.

_____

_____

_____

Marinate - Once you have chosen a verse, let it sink into your spirit. What thoughts or impressions do you feel the Holy Spirit is revealing to you?

_____

_____

_____

Ask- Ask God for clarity and wisdom as you finish up the day's reading. Ask what He would like you to do or improve. Ask Him for help if there is an area of need or a way you can bless someone else in need.

_____

_____

_____

Reveal- What has God revealed to you during this devotional time? Write down any thoughts or revelations.

_____

_____

_____

Take action- What is a practical step you can take after reading today's chapter or selected verse?

_____

_____

_____

#5Loaves2Fish

"Have you been asking God what He is going to do? He will never tell you. God does not tell you what He is going to do; He reveals to you Who He is."[17]

Oswald Chambers

I just knew the key to future stability and a comfortable retirement would come from my pursuing a degree in administration and then eventually becoming a principal. Looking at the annual income of a principal, plus the possibility of better pay raises, that was the path I felt I needed to be on. Plan, calculate, plan, get a little sidetracked then redirect, focus, and execute. That's pretty much how my brain seems to work. At that time, I was a mom to four sons (we now have five sons) and married to an enlisted soldier. We had a mortgage we could barely afford, daycare expenses that were never-ending, and bills that seemed to require most of our paychecks. I am not always the best at taking action, but I have always been a thinker and planner. I was certain going into administration for better pay (I know it's not always better pay and the workload is fierce, trust me) was the wisest and most efficient way to get ahead in life. However, I was also aware of my character, my heart, and my not-so-bold ways with people. I am well aware of how adults can act towards one another. I have seen the bickering and complaining that can happen between those in the trenches of teaching and those in administration. Heck, I know how we, as adults, can be petty with each other. We can get offended and have a hard time with corrections. We've all been there.

The more I started to realize that taking on a leadership position as a principal would entail dealing with these certain concerns, the more my mental projection didn't seem so appealing. I started to reflect on the gift and joy I had in teaching. To be honest, it was something that seemed like a natural flow for me. When I was in college, I majored in Psychobiology, certain I wanted to become a doctor. During my undergraduate years, I was a chemistry tutor. Even when I thought I wanted to be a physician, I was still teaching on the side. Looking back, I see that educating others has always been embedded in my heart. However, my persistent self was determined to figure out a way to increase our finances and have everything formulated for our future. I may have started to regress on my plans to pursue a career as an administrator, but that just left me open to a new master plan.

I carefully thought out strategic suggestions for my husband's future. I am telling you; I was relentless in trying to figure it all out. I remember quite clearly the many instances where I would ever so casually bring up the idea of him becoming an officer in the Army. The official term used was going 'green to gold.' That was the name of a program offered by the Army where an enlisted soldier could transition over to becoming an officer. I even remember trying to talk my friends who had experience in the program into bringing it up to my husband. I was using all my resources to help me with my idea. Each time, he would look at me and firmly respond, "I don't want to be an officer. I like what I do."
"Yes, I understand that, but look at the better pay. Isn't that more important?" I would counter reply.

Then, finally one day he said, "Why don't you go and be a principal, and then I will become an officer?" In that moment, I had a heart check. I didn't want to go into administration anymore because I realized that my gift, what I truly enjoyed doing, wasn't leading adults and overseeing a school, but being in the classroom helping develop young minds. Why was I pressuring my husband to switch over to a career he didn't feel called to do?

Money. Fear. Anxiety. All reasons that pushed me to overlook his wants. All reasons that convinced me to push for a career switch that possibly, in the long run, would have made us miserable. It could have even hurt the dynamics of our marriage and family. What if my marriage, kids, or family life couldn't handle that type of stress? What if that career move had required longer hours, hence missing out on more family time? I may have had the chance to make more money, but the sacrifice might not have been worth it. I wasn't thinking things through when I was planning out of fear and anxiety. I wasn't planning with God; *I was planning instead of God.* When I finally stopped trying to pave my own path (or the path of my husband), I was able to hear the Holy Spirit gently leading me to the story of Jesus feeding over 5,000 people in John 6:1-14.

In this story, Jesus is sitting on the mountainside with his disciples when He notices a large crowd coming toward them. His first response is to seek a way to feed the oncoming people. I love this reaction because it shows that our Lord and Savior cares about our provision, about meeting our physical needs here on Earth. He's not blind to our physical concerns and burdens. Jesus already knew how He was going to feed such a large crowd, but He asked one of His disciples where they could get bread to feed the people. He used this situation to teach the disciples, and us, several valuable truths. Andrew, Simon Peter's brother, tells Jesus a possible way to feed some of the people. He seems to reluctantly point out, "There is a little boy here who has five barley loaves and two fish; *but what are these for so many people?*" (John 6:9, AMP, emphasis added). How many times do we see our circumstances, possible financial hardships, or humble means, and think, *but what is this compared to all the demands and needs that exist?* Better yet, the actual concern: *this isn't enough!* Those five loaves and two fish were not enough to feed over 5,000 people. They weren't. I will not sugar coat or gloss over the reality; there is no possible way those loaves would have fed even one-tenth of the people there. But. God doesn't have limits to His wonder. In what seemed like a hopeless scenario, Jesus said,

> *"Have the people sit down [to eat]."Now [the ground] there was [covered with] an abundance of grass, so the men sat down, about 5,000 in number. Then Jesus took the loaves, and when He had given thanks, He distributed them to those who were seated; the same also with the fish, as much as they wanted. When they had eaten enough, He said to His disciples, "Gather up the leftover pieces so that nothing will be lost."*
> John 6:10-12, AMP

First, notice how Jesus responds to Andrew's dim perspective. Jesus immediately instructs the disciples to "have the people sit down and eat." Rather than giving a big lecture about their lack of faith or lack of remembrance for who He is, Jesus showed He is all about action, about taking our 'not enough' mentality and revealing His provision. He started with instructions. Their job was to be obedient, and His job was to provide the results. He took the meager resources, doubt, and uncertainty, and brought hope because He is our hope.

Have you ever been in a challenging situation where there seemed no viable positive outcome? Has God instructed you to do something? For me, many times when I am faced with financial hardship or I feel the pressures of the not so great paycheck of being a teacher, I need to be obedient in the instructions given in Proverbs 3:5-6 (AMP, emphasis added), "Trust in *and* rely confidently on the Lord with all your heart, and do not rely on your own insight *or* understanding. In all your ways **know** *and* **acknowledge** *and* **recognize** Him, and He will make your paths straight *and* smooth [removing obstacles that block your way]." Wow. Just take a moment and read those powerful instructions to us again. See, many times we can get so consumed with the poverty mentality, we don't do what God has initially instructed us to do: trust in Him, lean not in our own understanding, acknowledge (*know, recognize*) Him in all our ways, and then know He will make our paths straight and smooth.

When the disciples focused on their limited resources to feed the 5,000, it was easy to get discouraged looking with their physical eyes. Their first reaction was to look at temporal resources, rather than seek God for provision and help. Andrew, Simon Peter's brother, is a prime example of how many of us view our resources, questioning if what we have will be enough. Their solution to the need was not in Jesus, but what they could recognize, understand, and try to reason. However, when they turned to Jesus for an answer, He instructed them on what to do.

Friends, I understand each of us has our own personal struggles. Maybe, just like the disciples, you find yourself wondering how the little you have will be enough. Maybe the struggle isn't financial, but a limited view on what you know, lack of skills, experience, maybe just lack of belief. I've been there. I did all the planning and calculating I could to get myself out of financial concerns; I've tried to get through challenges with my own understanding. Each time, God had to slow me down and show me how to live at peace while I trusted Him for provision. I had to come to terms that the same God who supplied the needs of the hungry crowd could also supply the needs of my family, the needs of my wavering heart. Let us take time to draw first to the Lord for an answer rather than our own human understanding. This first step of following God's instructions (they are everywhere throughout the Bible) is important because it helps us not make rash decisions. Following His instruction helps us recognize He is in control, not us. It helps us to acknowledge that our answer will come from Him.

The second thing I notice from this passage is how God gave thanks for the seemingly little amount of food they had. Do I do that? Do you do that? Do we take time and thank God for what and where we are now, for the seemingly little things? Or, do we spend more time focusing on our wants and needs rather than on giving thanks? Friends, I still remember the feeling when I first got hired and signed my first contract as a teacher. I still have that paper. I remember how much I prayed to get that teaching job, how much I wanted to get hired and finally start working. And guess what? I got the job and felt so fortunate, so favored. But as with many things, the novelty wore off. The challenges of teacher life got to me, and the one thing I so desperately prayed for no longer was something I was thankful for. I went through a long period of time where I don't think I was thanking God for my career. Why? Because I had let the turmoil, complaints, and struggle make me look at my job as a burden rather than a blessing. When I forced myself to be thankful even when I didn't feel like it, I started to see how blessed I was to even have a job which provided some form of income. I was thankful God allowed me to be in a position where I was laughing with students who kept me feeling engaged and in tune with the youth experience. I started to see how being a teacher had actually helped me learn how to help my own kids at home. This intentionality to be thankful shifted my heart. I actually started to feel uncomfortable when I wanted to complain. It made me realize how other people really were struggling so much more and how I was failing to see the good in my life. That is a mental mindset, friends. That doesn't come naturally to any of us. We must be thankful, just as Jesus did when He lifted up the two fish and five loaves and gave thanks. He saw the abundance in what the Heavenly Father could do through so little.

When I finally understood this story and the powerful truth that nothing is too little, too small, or too insignificant in the hands of our mighty God, there was a sense of ease in my heart. A spring of hope and expectation started to arise inside of me, and I surrendered my ways to His ways. I started to actually believe that God could take my teacher's income and provide us with more than enough because the same God who multiplied the food for 5,000 could help multiply the provisions for my family of seven. I am not saying I became rich on paper, but I became richer in my knowledge of who God is. I started to gain priceless insight because I went from feeling weak and desperate to finding peace of mind. **Priceless**.

I don't know if anyone reading this has ever lost sleep worrying over things, but I have. What God gave me through this story was the encouragement I needed to trust Him with my resources, to seek Him for provision. When we read these stories in the Bible, we must recognize them for what they are: Biblical truths and recollections of great miracles Jesus did. The word says, "Jesus Christ is the same yesterday, today, and forever" (Hebrews 13:8, NLT). Let us find comfort that the same Jesus who supplied the needs of those around Him is still in the business of supplying all our needs. Let us take time and listen to His instructions, have a thankful heart, and be expectant for Him to move on our behalf like only He can. When I find myself getting restless, I repeat in my head: #5Loaves2Fish – "five loaves, two fish." It's always a great reminder of what He can do. It is a reminder of who He is, our Provider, our Way Maker.

POWER POINTS

John 6:9-12
Proverbs 3:5-6
Hebrews 13:8

POWER MOMENT

Jesus, thank You for being my ever-present help. Thank You for my current position and role. Please take my income, my resources, whatever I have, and help me give it back to You, trusting that You can do so much with whatever I have. When I feel like I have nothing to give, or my resources are lacking, please provide a source of financial, emotional, mental, and spiritual blessing. Lord, you care about all of me, my whole being. Please help me when I am struggling to believe and find rest. Bless my finances; help me to be wise with my resources and be a good steward of what I have. Help me rest and find peace of mind in You. Help me acknowledge You in all my ways and lean not on my own understanding. Lord, bless the works of my hands. I look to You for provision, abundance, and wisdom in all I do. In Jesus' name, amen!

SMART GOALS

Select - Choose a verse to meditate on. Write it below.

_____

_____

Marinate - Once you have chosen a verse, let it sink into your spirit. What thoughts or impressions do you feel the Holy Spirit is revealing to you?

_____

_____

_____

Ask- Ask God for clarity and wisdom as you finish up the day's reading. Ask what He would like you to do or improve. Ask Him for help if there is an area of need or a way you can bless someone else in need.

_____

_____

_____

Reveal- What has God revealed to you during this devotional time? Write down any thoughts or revelations.

_____

_____

_____

Take action- What is a practical step you can take after reading today's chapter or selected verse?

_____

_____

_____

#BehindtheScenes

"The decisions you make today will determine the stories you tell tomorrow."[18]

Craig Groschel

Time. I will confess I haven't made the best use of my time. I was once given an award at work entitled, "Ms. Focused Forgetful." It was fitting. Indeed, it was perfectly said. I have been known to get so zoned into my lessons, zoned into my routine, that deviating from my schedule could downright throw me in a tizzy. Anyone else have a hard time remembering to take attendance in the morning? Me too. (God bless all the attendance clerks who have had to hunt me down!) I don't like to stop what I am doing once I get started. I have learned over time to be more flexible, but the title Ms. Focused Forgetful is still fitting, even today. I am constantly asking God for help in the area of time management. I can put so much energy and focus in one area that I find it hard to remember other things that need to get done as well. As teachers, we are required to multitask. We are required to remember all sorts of dates, events, special occasions, last-minute meetings, handouts to pass out, the list goes on. The Lord seemed to impress on my heart that I needed to address how I was handling my pockets of time during the workday.

Sometimes we feel like there is not enough time to get everything done throughout our day. While I normally agree with this statement, I have realized that sometimes (hard to admit, again) I have been a poor steward of my time at work. What I am about to write might step on some toes, make you roll your eyes, or even cause you to think I am overreaching my boundaries, but hear me out. When it comes to our workday, hopefully, we work in a job where we have some 'planning time.' If you homeschool, you have the self-accountability to ensure some time is designated for certain subjects, including planning time, hopefully (we all know how hectic life can be). I understand it is different for all schools, teachers, and situations, but in general, we have been given these little pockets of time to help us gather our lessons, make copies, and do what needs to be done to help us throughout the day. I have worked in schools where individual planning times have ranged from thirty minutes to an hour a day. (There was only one year they gave us sixty minutes, unheard of, right?)

On many occasions, those planning times were just enough to run to the restroom, make copies, and frantically try to clear my guided reading table so I could pull a group when the students returned. However, there were also *numerous* times (where's the opened-eyed emoji face when you need one?) where I would be on my phone. No, not making important phone calls, that would be understandable. Instead, I was on my phone scrolling through social media, allowing valuable minutes to tick away. There were several instances where I would look at the clock and realize I had let my 'planning time' slip away. This little distraction of checking my phone and logging into social media engulfed my time more than I care to confess. Only after I felt a strong conviction from the Holy Spirit did I realize I was not being a good steward of my time. I reasoned with the Lord that after being so busy and on high gear with the demands around me, being on my phone or just scrolling through websites was my way of decompressing. But then it hit me, the time was given to me in my workday for planning and collaborating. What I was using it for did not align with what I should have been doing. Not using my time wisely made me feel even more rushed and disorganized. I was complaining about not having enough time to do things, yet when I was given time, I scrolled through social media. Earth to Gina, that doesn't make sense.

I am not sharing this to shame myself or to shame anyone else who may have found themselves in this contradiction of time management. I share this to be open and real with what I was doing and how it was negatively affecting my preparation and calmness during the day. I wanted to have time, but for some reason, I just couldn't get myself to focus on the things I needed to do. Can anyone else relate? I remember asking God to help me get more done throughout the day and His first tip...*put away your phone*. Ouch. You never really realize how much something has become a habit until you try to change it. I was convicted to be intentional and try not to get on my phone during designated planning times. If it was my lunch break, fine. But planning time, no. I felt such a strong conviction in my heart that I was wasting a valuable limited resource which was time.

Friends, this wasn't easy for me to do; I am still learning this skill. As soon as my class would leave or I was alone in my room, I found the sudden urge to pick up my phone. I had to make it a point during these prep/planning moments given to me to do as much as I could and not let my phone be a stumbling block. Before I continue, I want to clarify some things. Did this mean my conviction was law? No. I placed this charge on myself to improve my effectiveness at work, not to be legalistic or randomly place restrictions on myself.

We all know our habits and work routines. If you do not struggle with scrolling on your phone, great. However, I challenge you to check your use of time and see if there are any other things that may not be productive and can be minimized for more effective production with time. For me, not only was my phone a distraction, but so was my desire to socialize. Yes, I am the one who sometimes likes to wander and chit-chat (nothing wrong with that, unless our work doesn't get done, which for me was starting to occur more and more). When I asked God to help me to be more efficient with my time, He started showing me ways I could improve. Of course, I still talked with my coworkers; I love fellowship. I still used my phone now and then, but I intentionally tried to not let my own habits become my biggest setbacks. I started learning to be more self-aware, not allowing things to become time-suckers or distractions limiting me from being productive. Did I become the best at using my time wisely? No. Do I think it's worth striving for? Yes.

One resource we do not have the luxury to waste is…you guessed it, *time*. The Bible is full of advice when it comes to this commodity. Ephesians 5:15-17 (NLT, emphasis added) instructs, "So be careful how you live. Don't live like fools, but like those who are wise. *Make the most of every opportunity* in these evil days. Don't act thoughtlessly, but understand what the Lord wants you to do." The Amplified Bible digs deeper and reads, "recognizing and taking advantage of each opportunity and using it with wisdom and diligence." Diligence is defined as a "constant and earnest effort to accomplish what is undertaken; persistent exertion of body or mind"[19]. It requires effort. It is a conscientious choice to reflect and see what areas need improvement in order to give our most earnest effort. What we do behind the scenes may not be seen publicly, but it is evident by our visible actions. For me, effective time management in the *little* things makes the *biggest* difference in my productivity and mental calmness. Small adjustments throughout the day really do have a compound effect. Colossians 4:5b (AMP) tells us to, "Make the most of each opportunity [treating it as something precious]." Our time is precious, let us be mindful of it.

When you read the book of Ephesians, you will notice a common theme in Paul's writing. His goal was to encourage believers to imitate Christ, live in excellence, keep the unity in the body of believers, and live a Christ-inspired lifestyle. When we aim to imitate Jesus, it includes how we manage our time. Our days are fleeting. If we're not careful, we will fall into the trap of wasting moments, and indirectly cause more stress to ourselves later. I know there was and still is a huge need to improve in this area for me, but I am thankful for God's grace and help. We can't control our workload, but we can ask God for help to be effective with our time. He is as much in those big moments as He is in the small moments and details #behindthescenes.

If you have done your best at minimizing distractions, but still seem less diligent with time, seek out coworkers who appear to have a gift of organization and time management. I know you are already thinking of the person who is so efficient and on it. Maybe you are that person. Each of us has different talents and traits. I am always in awe of people who are organized and efficient. Learning what others do helps those of us who may just need some extra tips. Professional learning communities are not just about going over standards and activities. These learning communities are for us to grow in our teaching techniques, sharpen our skills, and find useful methods to help increase student performance. Teachers who share their expertise in topics such as time management and organization can enhance a teacher's craft and ability to better impact student learning. Maybe unlike me, you actually excel in this area. That is such a gifting. Maybe see this as just one way to model or help those around you who may struggle by sharing your time management strategies. Whether we are sharing our strategic systems or are on the other side of receiving the help, every little moment matters.

Lastly, I hate to admit this, but there is a high probability that even with all things set in place and time managed well, we will *still* feel behind and rushed. I recently started teaching a new grade level, and our 'planning time' is used for meetings and other discussions. The time that I would normally have been able to work in my room has now been occupied with filling out forms and discussing things I feel are not the best use of my time. #lesigh. I have even skipped eating lunch on numerous occasions (I do not encourage anyone to do this) because I am so busy trying to get ready for the remainder of the day. What I am trying to confess is, I get it. The struggle is real. I seriously wonder how any teacher can get it all done. But until a breakthrough happens with the workload educators juggle, I will do my best to be efficient, one moment at a time. I am still learning and feeling the pressures myself. Let's show ourselves grace as we make the best use of our time and not be so hard on ourselves when things aren't perfect or all done.

POWER POINTS

Ephesians 5:15-17
Colossians 4:5b

POWER MOMENT

Lord, thank You for being aware of my tendencies and human nature. Thank You that I can come to You with big requests and small requests, like helping me to manage my time better. Lord, help me to be more aware of my distractions, the things I do that are not beneficial to me at work or at home. Help me, God, to make the most of each opportunity. Bless the works of my hands. Help me with my lesson plans, timing things out, picking the best activities, and staying focused throughout my day. Lord, I give You my time; bless my moments and increase my reach and effectiveness in all I do. You know the never-ending demands, please help me do my best and have grace to move on. Instead of feeling like I can't do it all, help me seek You for wisdom to be productive. Give me Your peace and perspective of time so I can make the most of the day and enjoy it! In Jesus' name, amen.

SMART GOALS

Select - Choose a verse to meditate on. Write it below.

_____

_____

_____

Marinate - Once you have chosen a verse, let it sink into your spirit. What thoughts or impressions do you feel the Holy Spirit is revealing to you?

_____

_____

_____

Ask- Ask God for clarity and wisdom as you finish up the day's reading. Ask what He would like you to do or improve. Ask Him for help if there is an area of need or a way you can bless someone else in need.

_____

_____

_____

Reveal- What has God revealed to you during this devotional time? Write down any thoughts or revelations.

_____

_____

_____

Take action- What is a practical step you can take after reading today's chapter or selected verse?

_____

_____

_____

#TheFoundation

But blessed are those who trust in the Lord and have made the Lord their hope and confidence. They are like trees planted along a riverbank, with roots that reach deep into the water. Such trees are not bothered by the heat or worried by long months of drought. Their leaves stay green, and they never stop producing fruit.

Jeremiah 17:8, NLT

Pacing guides: the good, the bad, and the modifications I wish we used more. In my teaching experience, I have learned to see the value in pacing guides and actually think they are needed to keep educators grounded and on track. However, my actual teaching style is, at times, juxtaposed to a pacing guide's intended purpose. I start the year with the best intentions to stay right on track with lessons. I have high hopes to move seamlessly through English Language Arts and Math pacing timelines. I envision myself smoothly integrating engaging activities for the week and checking things off as they get accomplished. But, as life has it, with each new class, I tend to find the 'seamless' part rather difficult. As we all know, the beginning of the year is the time to set the stage for expectations, norms, best practices, and routines we hope our scholars will exemplify. The challenge with pacing guides is the expectation we set on the time frame. Time: there goes that word again. I realized early on the more time I took in the beginning to set a deep, solid foundation of fundamental skills, the smoother everything else seemed to fall into place. Not perfectly, but better. I believe that digging deeper into standards, skills, and strategies yields greater returns than trying to cover multiple concepts a mile wide.

A non-negotiable for me was making sure students made some form of progress (not all evident on paper). Many times, this aim would lead to my getting behind with the pacing guide. However, towards the middle/end of the school year, new material seemed to be grasped so much easier and more in-depth. Sometimes, we just need to slow down to speed up. At least that's one motto I remind myself. Maybe some students didn't meet mastery performance with me, but the goal was to get them as close as I could. Many times, there was no progress made according to state testing, but there was more progress in their attitude towards learning and trying. I wasn't perfect at this task, but I tried my best to make sure review, repetition, and new ways of learning were presented to help students understand things better. I can almost guarantee if you are reading this book now, you too have a heart of grit and hustle, meaning you want to do your best to ensure the success of those entrusted to you.

One error I found myself doing early on was trying to rush through certain topics just for the sake of keeping up with a pacing guide. I found myself not wanting to veer from my scheduled plans because it would throw everything else off. The problem I encountered with this mindset is that it wasn't centered around what was best for the students. Teaching is very complex. While some students may need to be challenged, there are those who need extra practice daily. I love this insight from Salman Khan, the developer of the free educational website Khan Academy. He states, "In a traditional academic model, the time allotted to learn something is fixed while the comprehension of the concept is variable...What should be fixed is a high level of comprehension, and what should be variable is the amount of time students have to understand a concept."[20] I do not have the perfect plan or perfect way to handle this dilemma of getting through standards and dealing with time constraints, but I do know where to start.

As believers, we have a priceless resource and wealth of knowledge from our God Almighty. I think we often fall back on logic, our own talents and abilities to get through things. Many times, it's in those seasons of not knowing how to do something that God shares His creativity. He is the creator of Heaven and Earth. How can we forget to seek Him to help us be creative in teaching as well? We may not all struggle with the timeline of pacing guides, but if you find yourself being in doubt, feeling behind, or just unsure because you are taking more time, don't worry, you are not alone. Teaching and learning are malleable, constantly developing and changing. What makes you a teacher at heart is your desire to meet the needs of your students and give your best. Being a teacher means we are also students constantly learning as well. Pacing guides keep us focused, but don't forget that time can be a variable.

I understand how demands are placed on us as educators. Many times, we cannot plan or give lessons as we choose. Some districts make it mandatory that all teachers be on the same lesson, same page, at the same time. I am not referring to this scenario. My prayer is, if you are in this situation, that things will change, and better yet, that God would bless you tremendously with favor and boldness to speak the truth with wisdom and insight, bringing change to your schools. I also pray that even with constraints around us, God would bless our planning and lessons to have even greater impact and effectiveness. For now, I write concerning my experience where I was blessed to have a little more wiggle room over the pace and lesson planning of my class. Regardless, I truly believe that digging deeper far outweighs covering too much too fast.

Just as pacing guides help keep us up to speed with learning targets for our students, we also have a resource in our walk with God that helps us keep in step with His Spirit. The Bible is our pacing guide without time constraints or boxed in restrictions (thank goodness). His word gives us clarity on *standards (our high calling)* and *objectives (aim)* we need to discover and learn. God's word not only guides our every step, but it encourages us to pause, dig deep, and connect with His heart, no matter how long it takes us. His word helps us know His character and attributes. Most of all, it draws us closer to what matters most in life, Him.

I have never done a one-year Bible reading plan. I don't think there is anything wrong with those plans, but I just so happen to be a slower learner, so reading the Bible in a year just hasn't happened yet. Things for me seem to take more time. In order for me to truly grasp what scripture says, I have to reread things, even read them in different translations, to get a better understanding. However, the extra time taken to study His word always helps to add a deeper layer of knowledge and a stronger foundation in my walk with Him. Just like I believe comprehension and digging deep is critical for learning objectives for my class, I believe being deeply rooted in His word is critical in our faith. Romans 10:17 (ESV) explains, "So, faith comes from hearing, and hearing through the word of Christ." Friends, as we plan to give our best in our careers, let's aim to give our best in learning His word. A Biblical foundation will help us not only increase our knowledge of Him, but to increase our expectation of what He can do on our behalf. If we're not careful, we can skim through our study of His word and miss out on fundamental insight that brings spiritual cognizance. Without a deep foundation, our understanding of things becomes harder. In teaching, we will face trials and hardships, but Proverbs 24:16, NLT explains,

"The godly may trip seven times, but they will get up again. But one disaster is enough to overthrow the wicked."

I don't recall having a year where I didn't fall or have setbacks. Sometimes, the setbacks are not in the classroom, they are happening in our personal life outside the work setting. However, as we all know, our personal, mental, and emotional health are what we bring to all aspects of our world, even our careers. When things seem to fall apart at home with my children or finances, it is God's word keeping me stable. It is His truths that get me up again, and it is God who will lift you up. The Bible is our anchor, and beautifully reminds us, "He will be the security *and* stability of your times, A treasure of salvation, wisdom and knowledge; The fear of the Lord is your treasure" (Isaiah 33:6, AMP). Did you take note of those two amazing words? *Security* and *stability*. Oh, how my heart and mind crave those things. He can and will give us those attributes because it is who He is: *secure* to depend on and *stable* not to let us down. Let us place our lives on His #FirmFoundation and make sure we make Him our treasure by getting rooted in His truth digging deep and studying His word. By studying His word, we obtain faith, and through faith, we believe His promises to us. We may stumble, even fall at times, but keeping Jesus as our foundation keeps us grounded and able to get back up, in Jesus' name!

POWER POINTS

Romans 10:17
Proverbs 24:16
Isaiah 33:6

POWER MOMENT

God, I thank You for being my why. Thank You for giving me a steady and firm foundation that I can base my hopes and dreams on. Lord, if there are things in my life hindering me from drawing closer to You, please help me set aside any stumbling blocks and pursue You as my great treasure. Please take my busy schedule and bring order. Take any pressures around me and bring ease of mind. Help me learn new and creative ways to challenge and enrich my students, while making sure to dig deeply into concepts with the time given to us. Lord, the demands may be heavy and hard at times, so I give them to You and ask for help and success in Jesus' name, amen.

SMART GOALS

Select - Choose a verse to meditate on. Write it below.

_____

_____

_____

Marinate - Once you have chosen a verse, let it sink into your spirit. What thoughts or impressions do you feel the Holy Spirit is revealing to you?

_____

_____

_____

Ask- Ask God for clarity and wisdom as you finish up the day's reading. Ask what He would like you to do or improve. Ask Him for help if there is an area of need or a way you can bless someone else in need.

_____

_____

_____

Reveal- What has God revealed to you during this devotional time? Write down any thoughts or revelations.

_____

_____

_____

Take action- What is a practical step you can take after reading today's chapter or selected verse?

_____

_____

_____

#PurposefullyPlanted

"The long way around isn't getting you nowhere. It's growing you somewhere."[21]

Lisa Whittle

I have a mantra I repeat in my head and even out loud at times: *I only have...* To be more specific it's more like: *I only have* 180 days left to make a difference. The number is a variable depending on how many days of instruction I have left with the students in my class. I repeat this because I believe in the impact a teacher can have on a person's life. If I leave my time up to chance and miss that truth, I might be counting down until summer rather than realizing that my presence in guiding those entrusted to me may be the only 'best' they get from someone. Don't get me wrong, of course I do the typical countdown to winter break and summer, but when I see my resolve to teach start to fade, I remind myself of my '*I only have*' mantra to check my perspective. It helps me remember that time is limited, and this current season is not forever. I say this to recognize the reality that we cannot guarantee tomorrow. We have no clue where our students will be next year, what will happen to their families, what type of teacher or other influence they will be exposed to after they leave our room. Maybe some of us don't have a set number of days, but we do have a set time frame regardless because days will pass and these moments will not physically last.

For the last twelve years, I have taught military children from across the globe. Within the school year, students leave sometimes in masses during PCS (Permanent Change of Station) season. I have witnessed students enter my class with a united family, only then to endure deployments, separation, and sometimes even divorce. Many times, I am the only constant they have in their life. Sometimes, I am the only source of guidance and direction they get for academic and behavioral support. This mentality has been a game-changer for me, especially on days I get ever so tired. I think about the world around us and how, when all is said and done, these students will face their own trials and challenges greater than a standardized test. Maybe, just maybe, the seeds I plant will be what they need to continue even when their hearts want them to stop.

Aside from being a schoolteacher, I am also the mother to five incredible, charming sons. They range in age from four to twenty-one years old. Talk about stretching my emotions thin at times. In a one-month time span, I witnessed my firstborn son graduate high school and prepare to leave our household (talk about all sorts of feels), while I simultaneously prepared to celebrate my youngest son's first birthday. I was closing a chapter in one story and starting a whole new book at the same time. There are no words to describe how parenting has changed my perspective on teaching, on what I do with those under my care.

Maybe you aren't a parent, but maybe you are an aunt, uncle, guardian, mentor, or elder to someone else and can agree that when we care for someone, we only want the best for them. If I want and expect nothing but the best given to my own kids as they attend school, how can I not give that same effort for the children of other parents? I have raised 'that kid' who struggles to pay attention in class. I have raised 'that kid' who is stubborn and can get bored easily. I have also raised 'that kid' who is a high achiever, but wants affirmation all of the time. I have raised 'that kid' who qualifies as gifted, but struggles with perfectionism and correction. And I have raised 'that kid' who got so behind in school that self-confidence hit an all-time low, and I didn't know what to do to help. Yes, even being a teacher myself, I have felt the strain of feeling like I failed my own kids at home. The pressure. The hurt. The overwhelming sadness. It aches.

I can recall countless times God has shown me traits in other people's children that were similar to my own children at home. I think about how I would want their teachers to respond to them, what reactions and interventions would be best utilized, but most of all, I think of compassion. I have lost my cool plenty of times, but what has increased my patience is realizing I must give what I want to receive. I want my children to have the best experiences in school, so I strive to give my best to those God has placed before me. There have been plenty of times where my attitude or reaction to a student has not been admirable. In those moments, I confess the Holy Spirit would remind me of one of my sons, to redirect me and guide me towards a better strategy. However, there have also been times where I did not respond appropriately and didn't feel convicted because my frustration was through the roof. But it never failed, sooner or later, I would find myself on the other end of the scenario. I would be the parent having one of my sons come home and tell me how something happened to him in his class, and it would convict me.

I will never forget one of my sons telling me how he didn't like his teacher. Not something a parent or teacher wants to hear. As any curious person or mother would, I asked why. He gave me the explanation that every morning in class, this particular teacher would direct students to do morning work and not ask questions until the allotted time was up. My son struggled in class and couldn't understand the work, so he said he tried asking the teacher for help (they were not allowed to talk or ask others in their group). He was redirected to sit down and get back to work. However, he noticed that when another student went up for help, the teacher worked with them and gave them time. For some reason, this incident really hurt his feelings, to the point when he was telling me about it, his eyes got watery, and he assumed the teacher just didn't like him. Now, bear with me friends; I understand how kids can be, how there could have been many other details he was leaving out, but it still got me thinking. Do I, as a teacher, sometimes make a student feel less favored? Do I show partiality to some students? Do I get so irritated with certain individuals that my tolerance to help them isn't the same as someone else? Do I give my best? Have I responded with the same care and attention I would want a teacher to give my own kids at school? Heart check.

I am convinced that God gave me five sons to humble me, refine me, and show me my constant need for His help and grace so I can show grace to others. It's so easy to be judgmental. It's so easy to think we have students, parents, and families figured out, but honestly, we will never have all the answers or know it all, and that's the way it's supposed to be. That constant unknown keeps us humble to seek the One who is constant: our heavenly Father. This job is essential to the growth and well-being of those around us. We get to impart traces of our moral compass, vision, and perspective to those who will be future leaders and contributors to our society. We also get to bring joy into the hearts of parents who worry and fear for their child's educational future and total wellbeing. You, my dear friend, get to bring peace and hope into the lives of others just by being your best you. The great gift God has given us in this line of work is the opportunity to positively influence the emotional, mental, and spiritual growth in every person we meet. We may not see the fruits right away, but we can sow the seeds and let God handle the rest.

I am reminded of Jesus' words. "You have not chosen Me, but I have chosen you and I have appointed *and* placed *and* purposefully planted you, so that you would go and bear fruit *and* keep on bearing, and that your fruit will remain *and* be lasting, so that whatever you ask of the Father in My name [as My representative] He may give to you" (John 15:16, AMP). We have been *appointed, placed and purposefully planted* where we are for a reason. We have not been placed in our classroom, our district, this moment, to dry and wither away. No, the word says we are to bear fruit and keep on bearing fruit. When we grasp the reality that God doesn't waste moments in our lives and each day has a significance, we can find worth and purpose in our job. We can change our outlook on things. We can use the struggle of teacher life to connect us more with Jesus rather than disconnect us from His presence. The teacher life struggle forced me to seek God in ways I probably never would have if things had been smooth sailing. Feeling helpless forced me to seek our great Helper. Getting connected with God provides us the greatest resource any person could ever have, constant support.

Jesus explains, "Get your life from Me and I will live in you. No branch can give fruit by itself. It has to get life from the vine. *You are able to give fruit only when you have life from Me*" (John 15:4, NLV, emphasis added). The saying, "We can't pour from an empty cup" is true, even the Bible says so! The reality is we do not have to pour from an empty cup. Will we get tired? Yes. Will there be days we feel like we just don't have anything left to give? Yes. Will there be hard days? Yes. But God didn't leave us helpless or hopeless. Friend, we have been given the gift of truth and the keys to unlimited times of refreshing and renewal through Him. Stay connected. Stay close. He is the One who will recharge our spirit. He is the One who will ignite our flame when it becomes a spark. He is the One who will take our #teachertired hearts and bring us back to life. Spiritual strength training from the best coach! The best part is that we will be able to bear fruit and serve because God never gets tired of refilling our cups. Remember His words, "You are able to give fruit only when you have life from Me." Check your life source; are you connected? If so, stay connected. If not, get plugged in and stay there.

I end this chapter with this: *We only have* these moments in life to bear fruit and make a difference. You have been #PurposefullyPlanted, to grow. Be intentional with your spiritual strength training. Stand firm in His word, drink from His living water, sharpen your swords, renew your minds, and stand on what is immovable, Jesus Christ our Lord and Savior. Commit your vocation and life to Him and believe He will do what He says in you and through you for His glory. Take the #teachertired life and start *teaching in truth*. Believe He can make you bloom where you're planted and bring you times of refreshing in Jesus' name!

POWER POINTS

John 15:16
John 15:4

POWER MOMENT

God, thank You for being intentional with me. Thank You that there is no detail in my life You do not know about or see. Whether I understand it all or know the next steps in my life, help me remember I am purposefully planted here for a reason. Help me live my life with intention and focus. Let this current season be one of great sowing and harvesting. Do not let me waste time worrying about my future or living in complacency. Keep my focus set on You and fill my cup with energy, motivation, joy, and positive expectation. God, only with You can I give my best and bear fruit. Help me stay rooted in You so I can be recharged, spiritually strengthened, eager to live my best life, and enjoy the learning moments with others. Keep me connected, growing, thriving, and bearing much fruit, in Jesus' name, amen!

SMART GOALS

Select - Choose a verse to meditate on. Write it below.

_____

_____

_____

Marinate - Once you have chosen a verse, let it sink into your spirit. What thoughts or impressions do you feel the Holy Spirit is revealing to you?

_____

_____

_____

Ask- Ask God for clarity and wisdom as you finish up the day's reading. Ask what He would like you to do or improve. Ask Him for help if there is an area of need or a way you can bless someone else in need.

_____

_____

_____

Reveal- What has God revealed to you during this devotional time? Write down any thoughts or revelations.

_____

_____

_____

Take action- What is a practical step you can take after reading today's chapter or selected verse?

_____

_____

_____

#SpiritualStrengthTraining

I want to leave you with final words that have been echoing in my heart: "Now it's time to be made new by every revelation that's been given to you" (Ephesians 4:23, TPT).

Forming new habits, building strength, making any kind of progress requires action. Practice. Consistency. We've searched through scripture together, each page revealing spiritual truths that strengthen our spirit. Now is the time to take the revelations given to you and be renewed. Spiritual strength training never stops; continue in your walk with the Lord and let His words refresh your soul. I pray this over every person reading these words:

May the Lord bless you
and protect you.
May the Lord smile on you
and be gracious to you.
May the Lord show you his favor
and give you his peace.
Numbers 6:24-26 (NLT)

#Continue #TeacherStrong #TeachinginTruth

#References

1) Lewis, C. S. The Abolition of Man. New York, NY: HarperOne, 2009.

2) Merriam Webster. "Purpose," accessed April 10, 2020, https://www.merriam-webster.com/dictionary/purpose.

3) Muggeridge, Malcolm. Christ and the Media. Vancouver, BC: Regent College Publishing, 2003.

4) Tozer, A.W. The Knowledge of the Holy. New York, NY: HarperCollins, 1978.

5) Tolkien, J.R.R. The Fellowship of the Ring. New York, NY: Houghton Mifflin, 1994.

6) Myers, Michelle. (March 2019). She Works His Way [webinar].

7) Lewis, C.S. Letters of C. S. Lewis. New York, NY: HarperOne, 2017.

8) Graham, Billy. Hope for the Troubled Heart: Finding God in the Midst of Pain. Nashville, TN: Thomas Nelson, 2011.

9) Blanchard, Ken, and Spencer Johnson. The One Minute Manager: Increase Productivity, Profits, and Your Own Prosperity. New York, NY: HarperCollins, 1982.

10) Ravi Zacharias International Ministries, INC. "RZIM." Ravi Zacharias International Ministries, INC., 2.7.6 (2016). rzim.org (accessed on February 17, 2017).

11) Stanley, Andy. 2020. "Your beliefs shape your attitude." Accessed July 10, 2020. https://www.azquotes.com/quote/443773.

12) Elliot, Elisabeth. Quest for love. Grand Rapids, MI: Baker Publishing Group, 2002.

13) Spurgeon, Charles. 2020. "It's not how much we have, but how much we enjoy, that makes happiness." Accessed July 10, 2020. https://www.brainy-quote.com/quotes/charles_spurgeon_131342.

14) Shadowlands. Richard Attenborough. United Kingdom: Paramount Pictures, 1993.

15) Hutchings, Lucy. "Margaret Thatcher's Most Famous Quotes." Vogue. Accessed April 5, 2020, https://www.vogue.co.uk/gallery/margaret-thatcher-most-famous-quotes?image=5d54558e12e31a00084809a8.

16) Mason, Babbie, and Eddie Carswell, "Trust His Heart," 1989, track #8 on Timeless, Spring Hill, 2001, compact disc.

17) Chambers, Oswald. "Will You Go Out Without Knowing?" My Utmost for His Highest, accessed April 9, 2020, https://utmost.org/will-you-go-out-without-knowing/.

18) Groeschel, Craig. Daily Power: 365 Days of Fuel for Your Soul. Grand Rapids, MI: Zondervan, 2017.

19) Dictionary.com. "Diligence," accessed April 10, 2020, https://www.dictionary.com/browse/diligence.

20) Khan, Salman. The One World Schoolhouse: Education Reimagined. New York, NY: Grand Central Publishing, 2012.

21) Whittle, Lisa (@lisawhittle). 2019. "The long way around isn't getting you nowhere. It's growing you somewhere." November 20, 2019. https://instagram.com/lisawhittle?igshid=1s908yi9nhreu.

#AboutTheAuthor

Gina Rodriguez is a military spouse and mom to five sons and one daughter. With a Master's degree in Education and an EDS in Curriculum & Instruction, her heart's passion is to serve and help students grow in all aspects of learning. Her motto "healthy from the INSIDE out" is evident in her approach to teaching the whole person. If she's not busy trying to keep up with laundry, finding new and easy recipes for her Instapot, or reading, you will most likely find her at the gym strength training. Teaching is a talent that she has learned to see as a gift from God. She aims to serve and encourage educators to see the Word of God as a valuable resource for professional development. Gina currently resides at Fort Bragg, NC.

You can learn more about her @ginarodriguez316, www.facebook.com/memyselfandtheone